IBN KHALDUN'S SOCIOLOGICAL THOUGHT

Ilm al-umran is "an independent science. This science has its own peculiar object — that is, human civilization and social organization. . . . The discussion of this topic is something new, extraordinary, and highly useful. Penetrating research has shown the way to it."

Ibn Khaldun

SOCIETY, STATE, AND URBANISM:
IBN KHALDUN'S SOCIOLOGICAL THOUGHT

Fuad Baali

State University of New York Press

Published by
State University of New York Press, Albany

Printed in the United States of America

For information, address State University of New York
Press, State University Plaza, Albany, N.Y., 12246

Library of Congress Cataloging-in-Publication Data

Baali, Fuad.
    Society, State, and Urbanism: Ibn Khaldun's Sociological Thought.

    Bibliography: p.
    Includes index.
    1. Ibn Khaldun, 1332-1406. Kitab al-'Ibar.
Muqaddimah.   2. Civilization.   3. Sociology, Urban.
I. Title.
D16.7.I26B25   1988   909.07   87-9925
ISBN 0-88706-609-7
ISBN 0-88706-610-0 (pbk.)

10   9   8   7   6   5   4   3   2   1

For My Daughter
JASMINE

— Summarize the reading passage and then relate to what Khaldulc says in the book

CONTENTS

PREFACE

Published works on Ibn Khaldun may be classified into four categories: (1) the very "pro," which glorifies Ibn Khaldun's *Muqaddimah* as an intellectual miracle — an inexplicable stroke of genius, without which "nothing would be left in the Arabic heritage that deserves to be called a science or a social study";[1] (2) the extreme "con," which declares that Ibn Khaldun did not make any contribution to our knowledge and that his *Muqaddimah* "is a curiously twisted, grand misconception of the historical process";[2] (3) the "encyclopedic," which gives no judgment — Ibn Khaldun's work speaks for itself; and (4) the invented, which attributes to Ibn Khaldun ideas and theories that he never made.[3]

This volume follows none of the above categories. It does not indiscriminately praise everything Ibn Khaldun wrote in his *Muqaddimah*, nor does it criticize his whole work in a few dogmatic statements. Furthermore, it refrains from assigning any idea to him that is not found in his work; such an activity is unethical and unprofessional. This study endeavors to present and evaluate Ibn Khaldun's ideas objectively. To quote him: "Little effort is being made to get at the truth . . . . No one can stand up against the authority of truth, and the evil of falsehood is to be fought."[4]

Several writers believe that Ibn Khaldun was the first to lay down the foundation of what we call sociology, and accordingly he is "the first sociologist" and "the father of sociology."[5] However, none of these writers presented a detailed explanation to convince their readers of Ibn Khaldun's contributions. A detailed, comprehensive, and *documented* study is needed. Hopefully, this treatise will satisfy that need; and by emphasizing the sociological perspective of this Arab thinker's contributions, the challenges and rewards that can accompany such a work will be realized.

The arguments presented herein are based on two points: (1)   Ibn Khaldun himself realized that he had established a new science; and (2)   large portions of his contributions are relevant today, and his very language differs little from that of classical and modern sociologists. That is, the link between Ibn Khaldun and other social thinkers is primarily a *conceptual*, rather than a historical, one.

Admittedly, some of the data in Ibn Khaldun's *Muqaddimah* are not related to his new science. The same is true of Comte's *Positive Philosophy*, which contains large sections unrelated to sociology.[6] Furthermore, because Ibn Khaldun's work represents the writing style of his era, I had to reassemble his contributions from bits here and there in his *Muqaddimah*.

Arguably, Ibn Khaldun belongs to the fourteenth century and, hence, should not be studied in the light of "modern" thought. In this work, Ibn Khaldun is seen against his medieval background, and accordingly some of his generalizations are not applicable today. However, this should not prevent one from selecting those segments of his work that currently appear relevant, and that can be compared with "modern" and recent thought. In this case, neither are Ibn Khaldun's ideas exaggerated nor are modern writings belittled. One major task of the sociologist is to identify the similarities in different events at different times. Through this approach, one can arrive at verifiable information that may serve as grounds for prediction. That is, if some of Ibn Khaldun's ideas help one to formulate accurate (scientific) theory about human social organization, then they ought not to be ignored. In science, the connections between the different stages of its development are not overlooked.

Contemporary sociologists consider Auguste Comte, Herbert Spencer, Georg Simmel, and Max Weber sociologists. However, Comte used "society" and "humanity" interchangeably; and his writings, as will be seen, are regarded as "dogmatic." "Like Comte, Spencer was essentially a philosopher."[7] In the chapter on "The Scope of Sociology" in his *Study of Sociology*, Spencer "covered completely the field now generally allotted to political science"; and the book itself has "perhaps a misleading title."[8] Simmel also "was primarily a philosopher whose interests were not at all confined to the problems of society."[9] And, in one of his publications, Max Weber considered himself a "political economist."[10] While one discovers that some of the "fathers" and "pioneers" of sociology are not considered sociologists, one also realizes that some six centuries ago Ibn Khaldun declared that he had founded "the science of human social organization," which is independent from philosophy, political science, and other disciplines, and which is very much equivalent to what is now called sociology.

Following Chapter 1, which concerns Ibn Khaldun's life and work, the book may be divided into three parts. The first part (Chapters 2 and 3) deals with the nature, scope, and methods of Ibn Khaldun's new science "of social organization." The second part (Chapters 4 through 6) can be considered a unit dealing with the Khaldunian cyclical theory. *Asabiyah* is regarded as the seed that leads to the rise and fall of the state. The third part (Chapters 7 and 8) is concerned with the ways of life, especially urbanism.

With the exception of this author's own translation of a few paragraphs from Ibn Khaldun's *al-Muqaddimah*, Franz Rosenthal's excellent translation, *The Muqaddimah: An Introduction to History* (Princeton: Princeton University Press, 1967), is used in this volume to trace Ibn Khaldun's thought.

The gratitude of the author is expressed to H. Kirk Dansereau for reading the manuscript and making invaluable remarks; to the several anonymous reviewers for their helpful and encouraging comments; to Elashia J. Martin and Linda B. Baali for typing the manuscript; and to the State University of New York Press for making possible the publication of this book.

F. G. Baali
Bowling Green, Kentucky

Chapter 1

THE MAN
AND HIS BACKGROUND

I. Ibn Khaldun's Life and Character

Abu Zaid Abdalrahman ibn Muhammad ibn Khaldun Wali-
ad-Din al-Tunisi al-Hadrami was born in Tunis (Tunisia) on May
27, 1332. He was brought up in a family known for its activities
in both learning and politics. His Arab ancestors, Banu
Khaldun, beginning with Khaldun bin al-Khattab, moved to
Andalusia (Spain) in the eighth century and, thus, witnessed the
growth and decline of Spanish Muslim power. They left for
Morocco just before the fall of Seville in 1248.

Ibn Khaldun's homeland, fourteenth-century North Africa,
was characterized by a depressed intellectual life and continuous political instability. The Arab Muslim Empire had
already declined; and, as a result, small states succeeded one
another. Rivalries, intrigues, plots, and upheavals were common features of political life and a fertile arena for ambitious
power seekers.

In this environment, the Arab Muslim Ibn Khaldun had his
basic education in religion, philology, poetry, logic, and
philosophy. The education he received from his teachers seems
to have been thorough and scholastic.[1]

Ibn Khaldun entered into public life before having attained
age twenty. His first position was that of the seal bearer. He said
he accepted that post reluctantly because he considered it inferior, for none of his ancestors had occupied it. His ambitious

desire for greater authority and power, *e.g.*, premiership, motivated him to engage in political intrigues and conspiracies, pitting one ruler against another; a behavior that led him to spend two years in prison (1357–1358). When Ibn Khaldun regained his freedom, he resumed his political activity. One year later, he occupied the positions of secretary of state and judge. In 1362, he joined the court of the Muslim ruler of Granada. Remembering how useful Ibn Khaldun had been to him and to his prime minister Ibn al-Khatib when they were in Fez (Morocco) as fugitives, the ruler gave Ibn Khaldun a friendly reception. He was now sent as an ambassador to the court of Pedro the Cruel of Castile to ratify a peace treaty between the two states. The Christian ruler not only honored Ibn Khaldun, but also tried to win him over to his side by offering him the former estates of the Khaldun family in Seville. Ibn Khaldun declined. In Granada, however, Ibn al-Khatib was displeased with Ibn Khaldun's increasing power in the court. At that time, Ibn Khaldun was happy to receive, and to accept, an offer from the North African Hafside ruler to be his prime minister.

After having changed sides from ruler to ruler, Ibn Khaldun felt tired of political adventures. He abandoned politics and sought refuge among the Banu Arif tribe. It was there he composed his famous *Muqaddimah*, his *Prolegomena to History.*

Having written *The Muqaddimah*, Ibn Khaldun grew tired of the seclusion. To break the monotony of retirement, he aspired to return to Tunis, his birthplace. He wrote the Tunisian ruler an emotional letter, explaining why (some ten years earlier) he had incited tribes against his rule. Ibn Khaldun pleaded for the sultan's forgiveness and asked for his permission to let him come to Tunis to do some scholarly work. The sultan consented.

The tranquility which Ibn Khaldun enjoyed in his old home did not last long. Some of his friends intrigued against him. In addition, the sultan ordered the thinker to accompany him in fighting some insurgents. Ibn Khaldun began to resent these dangerous missions and decided to go on a pilgrimage. He left Tunis in 1382, for Alexandria, Egypt. To continue his journey to Mecca he had to go to Cairo, a city that previously impressed him enormously.

In Cairo, Ibn Khaldun adopted a teaching role. Students crowded his "mosque-circle" and were enchanted by his eloquent explanations of social phenomena.[2] Afterwards, and after hesitation, he accepted an appointment as a judge; but he did not go back to his old habit of exploiting public offices to further personal ends. He proceeded in his judicial practices with strict honesty and great integrity.[3] It seems, however, that his impartial administration made him many enemies. In 1384, he resigned his post after the sad news reached him that his family, who were coming from Tunis to join him, had become the victims of a shipwreck near Alexandria. Ibn Khaldun turned again to teaching and accepted an appointment as professor of jurisprudence at the Egyptian Zahiriyah College. In 1387, he finally was able to go to Mecca. After the pilgrimage, he was appointed president of Baybars Institute in Egypt, a post he had to relinquish soon after he and some legal authorities had issued a proclamation against the sultan of Egypt. In 1389, he became a Malikite (religious) judge for the second time. During this period, he had an opportunity to visit Palestine.

In 1400, the Tatar army under the leadership of Timur (Tamerland) invaded Syria. The ruler of Egypt hastened with his army to move against the invaders. He asked Ibn Khaldun to accompany him on this expedition. When they arrived in Syria, the sultan learned about a plot to dethrone him. He quickly returned to Egypt, leaving Ibn Khaldun in the besieged Damascus to recommend negotiations with the Tatar leader. The latter wanted to see Ibn Khaldun, and accordingly a meeting was arranged. They had a long discussion about political affairs during which the Arab thinker was asked to write a treatise about North Africa, which he did. Afterwards he returned to Egypt, where he wrote a detailed account of his meetings with Timur, and a copy of this work was sent to the sultan of Tunis.

Ibn Khaldun died on March 16, 1406, shortly after his sixth nomination for the judgeship. He was buried in the Sufi (Sufite) cemetery in Cairo.

Ibn Khaldun seemed to be the only writer in the history of Islam who, with an amazing frankness, wrote a detailed book about his secular activities. In his *Autobiography*, he flatly and

without any apology told of the flattering and fickleness of his
political life. In this respect, the *Autobiography* was considered
an astonishing and inexplicable phenomenon to his contemporary fellow writers. Until now, no one has been able to
explain fully why Ibn Khaldun dared to write this candid book
about himself.[4] Ibn Khaldun appeared to be an admirer of the
pharisaical wisdom that "where all are at fault, none is at fault."
He was not ashamed of his behavior because he believed that
all men are fickle and flatter in one way or another. Schmidt
erred when he said that to the end of his life Ibn Khaldun "continued to use the mammon of unrighteousness to further personal ends."[5] Several writers have defended Ibn Khaldun by
pointing out that even his bitterest enemies in Egypt
acknowledged his honesty as a judge. Al-Sakhawi, one of Ibn
Khaldun's most severe critics, declared that Ibn Khaldun "was
well-known by the maintenance of justice."[6] In contrast to
Schmidt, von Wesendonk believed that the whole life of Ibn
Khaldun, from the beginning to the end, was sincerely devoted
to the search for knowledge; he was always an honest, sincere,
and high-principled man.[7] Schmidt and von Wesendonk each
appeared to concentrate upon a different part of Ibn Khaldun's
life and overlooked the other part. The fact is that Ibn Khaldun
was both fickle and sincere – fickle before the withdrawal
(seclusion among Banu Arif tribe), sincere after it.

One of the interesting aspects of Ibn Khaldun's life was his
intimate relationship and close friendship with both religious
scholars and tribal chieftains. Ibn Khaldun was particularly
liked by the tribal leaders and was influential among them.
Husri attributed this fact to his penetrating eloquence, which
encouraged some rulers to attract him to their side.[8] His keen
understanding of the values of tribal chieftains was also effective. Eloquence without understanding and knowledge may
give the impression of superficiality and pendantry; it may
distract rather than attract an audience. It is amazing, indeed,
to find that Ibn Khaldun was able to attract not only tribal chieftains, who spoke the same language as he did, but also Pedro the
Cruel, the king of Castile, and Timur (Tamerlane) the Lame.

II. Ibn Khaldun's Work

With the exception of the Introduction and Book One (*The Muqaddimah*) of the World History (*Kitab al-Ibar*), the rest of Ibn Khaldun's works are not relevant herein.[9]

Ibn Khaldun's *Muqaddimah*, which is based on his rich experience, seems to generate different and conflicting views. This may be the problem of any work viewed through a perspective different from that of the author, that is, from an angle or a viewpoint with which the author is not familiar. Truth is a highly complicated phenomenon, impossible to be seen entirely from a single perspective.[10] Truth may be likened to a multifaceted pyramid. No one is able to see all of its sides (or triangular faces) at the same time while standing in one place. The truth can be grasped, as Mannheim has pointed out, only through a roundabout fashion, *i.e.*, through a generalized view that synthesizes all the various particular views.[11]

Hussein's and de Slane's complaint about the vagueness of, and the contradictions in, Ibn Khaldun's writings[12] cannot be easily accepted. Ibn Khaldun is far from being contradictory; and his writing is very clear in comparison with that of the other writers of his time and culture. The so-called vagueness may be attributed to the fact that de Slane studied Ibn Khaldun from the static viewpoint, whereas Ibn Khaldun looked at social phenomena from the dynamic viewpoint. To Ibn Khaldun, the very same thing can be good and bad, useful and harmful. He praised the Arabian nomads and declared at the same time that they were "savage" people.[13] Using Ibn Khaldun's perspective, then, savageness is a way of life, a way of thinking and behaving; it may not have a bad connotation; it may mean the same as manliness, bravery, liberty, pride, and the like. In his terminology civilization may connote softness, "womanliness," cowardliness, humiliation, and so on, qualities he considered defects in man.[14]

Erwin Rosenthal asserts that "Ibn Khaldun was a Muslim, and must be seen against the background of Medieval Islam if we are to understand his teaching." He adds that although one can find in Ibn Khaldun's work striking parallel with ideas of European thinkers from the eighteenth century onward, one must not see in him a precursor of these thinkers, be they Vico, Comte, Hegel, Marx, or Spengler. "If a comparison must be made, we can still think of no closer parallel in matters political than Machiavelli."[15] In response to this statement it can be said that although Ibn Khaldun was a Muslim, Islam should not be taken as the only determinant of his thought. Some of his generalizations are not necessarily influenced by Islamic thoughtstyles. Even though his main observations were in North Africa and in southern Spain, he nevertheless utilized information on other places and of non-Islamic groups. His emphasis on North Africa is a parallel with the emphasis of Marx, Spengler, Comte, Spencer, and several others on social and economic conditions in industrial European countries that have formed the principal subject matter of Western sociology.[16] Does this mean that these thinkers must be seen only against the background of European Christianity if one is to understand their contributions? Moreover, because Plato and Aristotle are frequently compared with modern and contemporary writers, it seems possible, if not "logical," to compare Ibn Khaldun with Vico, Spengler, Marx, Comte, and others. Furthermore, Ibn Khaldun's *ilm al-umran* (Chapter 2) is the study of social organization or civilization that concerns more than just "political" matters. Even if his analysis of political life is studied in relation to society's structure, one finds that he followed an *independent* approach.[17] Rosenthal is correct in comparing Ibn Khaldun with Machiavelli. Ibn Khaldun can be rightly considered the Islamic version of Machiavelli. Both thinkers distinguished themselves from their scholastic contemporaries by treating social affairs within a highly realistic frame of reference. Nevertheless, a major difference exists between the two that should not be overlooked. Whereas Machiavelli rejected idealism for realism, Ibn Khaldun acknowledged the validity and importance of both. To Ibn Khaldun, what *ought to be* is as valid as what *is*, but they should be separated, each to be placed in its special realm and prevented from interfering with the other.

Now Ibn Khaldun's connection with philosophy and history is discussed. Was Ibn Khaldun a disciple of classical and Islamic philosophies? Mahdi asserts that the Arab-Muslim thinker attempted to develop a science of social organization "within the framework of traditional philosophy and based on its principles," and that he "sided with the purely philosophic tradition of Islamic thought, the tradition of Farabi, Avicenna, and Averroes."[18] Simon also believes that the ties that unite Ibn Khaldun with predecessors are strong and determine his basic philosophical position, for he shows a clear agreement with the Muslim Aristotelians, especially Averroes.[19]

The preceding statements cannot be accepted in their entirety. It is a truism that Greek philosophy had a great impact upon Islamic thought. It is also true that Ibn Khaldun rejected the abstract, speculative philosophy:

> There are certain intelligent representatives of the human species who think that the essences and conditions of the whole of existence, both the part of it perceivable by the senses and that beyond sensual perception, as well as the reasons and causes of these essences and conditions, can be perceived by mental speculation and intellectual reasoning. They also think that the articles of faith are established as correct through intellectual speculation and not through tradition because they belong among the intellectual perceptions. Such people are called "philosophers." . . . It should be known that the opinion the philosophers hold is wrong in all its aspects . . . . The insufficiency lies in the fact that conformity between the results of thinking – which, as they assume, are produced by rational norms and reasoning – and the outside world, is not unequivocal.[20]

According to philosophers, Ibn Khaldun added, logic enables "intellectual speculation to distinguish between true and false."[21] However, "logic is not adequate to achieve the avowed intentions of the philosophers." It "cannot be trusted to prevent the commission of errors, because it is too abstract and remote from the *sensibilia*."[22] Ibn Khaldun did not ignore the fact that logic has merit, in that it helps one present orderly proofs and arguments; but this traditional logic was a useful tool of attack and defense in the hands of conflicting groups. Furthermore, logic does not produce knowledge.[23] Had he followed the rules of the Aristotelian logic, he would not have been able to develop his "science of social organization" (ilm al-umran), which accepts only the actual logic of the events themselves, i.e., the logic that can be verified. (See Chapter 2.) This explains why he tried to find the actual laws which govern societal processes.[24] The question that must be answered here is: Where and how did Ibn Khaldun find the starting point of his social theory? According to some writers, Ibn Khaldun was a Ghazzalian;[25] according to others, he was a Rushdian.[26] This may sound strange considering that al-Ghazzali and Ibn Rushd (Averroes) were opposed to each other in their philosophical orientation. While Ibn Rushd was the most ardent student and admirer of Aristotle in Islam, al-Ghazzali was his most bitter enemy.[27] We believe that Ibn Khaldun can be regarded as Ghazzalian and Rushdian at the same time. He adopted from al-Ghazzali his hostility toward Aristotelian logic, and at the same time adopted Ibn Rushd's (Averroes') favorable attitude toward the masses.[28]

Simon admits that Ibn Khaldun "does not consider himself a philosopher at all,"[29] and that he "separates himself from subjective idealism on one hand, and from speculative rationalism on the other."[30] In fact Simon believes that "with the exception of his agreement with the Aristotelian view of man as a political being, Ibn Khaldun did not rely on the authority of any of his predecessors in the development and explanation of his theory."[31]

Briefly, Ibn Khaldun was not satisfied with philosophy and its logical deductions that frequently do not correspond with his actual observations of human social organization and social change.[32] Indeed, one can find in his new science, ilm al-umran, some philosophic ideas and concepts. This is also true of Comte's Positive Philosophy and of sociology in general. The interrelation of some sciences is expected and should not hamper the status of any of them.

As for Ibn Khaldun's connection with history, he saw history as a useful discipline that deals with civilization.[33] History is not a mere succession of events but a natural process that explains the continuity of historical development, a view quite different from the customary interpretation of history at his time, and he here anticipated Vico and Turgot.

Like Vico and Comte, Ibn Khaldun's basic thesis was to *interpret history in terms of group changes.* Ibn Khaldun criticized tradition-bound historians who "disregard the changes in conditions and in the customs of [people] that the passing of time had brought about."[34] Some scholars believe that what Ibn Khaldun meant by history is in actuality a philosophy of history.

Although he is considered by Sorokin, Flint, Barnes, Schmidt, de Boer, Simon, Watt, Enan, and Khalife[35] the founder of a scientific history, Ibn Khaldun believed that the *inner* meaning of history "involves speculation . . . and therefore is firmly rooted in philosophy. It deserves to be accounted a branch of philosophy."[36]

Chapter 2

THE NEW SCIENCE:
ILM AL-UMRAN

This chapter proves that some six centuries ago Ibn Khaldun
founded a "science of social organization" similar to what is now
called sociology. The nature, scope, and methods of this new
science are discussed herein in detail. Despite some divergen-
cies, Ibn Khaldun and Comte converge in their methodology
and in some other aspects of their writings.

    The question of when sociology emerged has engaged the
minds of many writers. Three views exist: (1) that sociology,
as Small stated, could not and did not emerge in isolation from
other related social sciences that faced and solved some of the
most crucial problems of sociology before Comte gave it a
name; (2) that, as Giddings pointed out, a new sociological
approach to studying social phenomena was predicted if not
created by Comte;[1] and (3) that sociology did not emerge
before the fourth quarter of the nineteenth century, and that it
"as a clearly defined, independent social science is only today
coming into existence."[2] This third view does not ignore the contributions of early thinkers, including those of the Middle Ages,
to the history of the science.[3] The first two views are predominant; they are also pertinent to this chapter.
    It is generally acknowledged that Auguste Comte
(1798–1857) is "the father of sociology," or "the father of modern
sociology,"[4] which he defined as an abstract science "of society,"[5]

"of social phenomena,"[6] of social order (or structure) and social progress (or dynamics).[7] He sought sociology's emancipation from theological and metaphysical conceptions so that it may discover the laws that regulate social phenomena. That is, sociology needs the *positive* method, which is not necessarily identified with using quantitative techniques. Positivism maintains that concepts and methods used in the natural sciences can be applied to social phenomena. To study social phenomena, four methods may be used: observation, experiment, comparison, and historical procedure.[8]

Comte's "positivism"[9] was a "science," and a "religion for humanity," by which he aimed for a complete reorganization and improvement of human society. He did not define the concept of society, nor did he make a clear distinction between sociology and political science.[10] Tönnies believed that "Comte's sociology almost immediately turned into philosophy of history"; and that it "reveals his lack of a clear scientific conception."[11] A similar comment was expressed by Durkheim.[12]

Comte acknowledged the contributions of Montesquieu and Condorcet.[13] His intellectual debt to those two thinkers and to Aristotle, Saint-Pierre, and Saint-Simon leads one to the often-debated question of his originality.[14] Specifically, his intellectual relationship with Claude Henri de Saint-Simon (1760–1825) demands some explication. Saint-Simon is considered a utopian social thinker who believed that the welfare of humanity required the reorganization of human society, including the means of production. His 1813 *Memoire sur la Science de l'home*, published in 1859, specified the positive program long before Auguste Comte became his secretary. Their collaboration (1817–1823) resulted in their treatise, *Plan of the Scientific Operations Necessary for the Reorganization of Society.* Soon after the publication of this work, their partnership was dissolved. By 1830, Comte had quarrelled violently with the Saint-Simonians, and, as some writers have indicated, "tried to suppress all evidence of the great influence which Saint-Simon had had on his thought." Saint-Simon's fundamental doctrines indicate that the sciences must be classified in the order of their increasing complexities, and a new science, *la science politique,* must be put at the head of the hierarchy. This science is based on the inductions of history and observation, and must be animated by the conception of progress.

The contention that Comte's early ideas were not particularly his own, led some writers to believe that Montesquieu was much more of a sociologist than Auguste Comte.[16] In fact, Durkheim repeatedly stated that "Montesquieu . . . laid down the principle of the new science."[17] In such arguments, Ibn Khaldun's new science is seldom acknowledged. Sociology texts, including those designed for classrooms, normally do not mention Ibn Khaldun's, for that matter any Arabic-Islamic, contribution to sociology. As an example, one text devotes a section to the "early scientific work on society," describing the works of Plato and Aristotle as the first period of "scientific sociology"; the second period "began in the sixteenth century with the development of secular social thought."[18] On the other hand, there are some social scientists, especially sociologists such as Pitirim A. Sorokin, Ludwig Gumplowicz, Harry Elmer Barnes, and Howard Becker, whose writings emphasize the Arabic contribution to sociology. Sorokin considered Ibn Khaldun's *Muqaddimah* "the earliest systematic treatise both in sociology and in rural-urban sociology."[19] Ibn Khaldun has been called the "father of sociology," "the founder of sociology," and a "sociologist."[20] These characterizations of Ibn Khaldun and his his work were made without tangible efforts to examine in greater detail his original writings, hence the work herein provides such supportive evidence.

I. Ibn Khaldun's New Science

Ibn Khaldun himself was well aware of his accomplishment. He thought of his work *The Muqaddimah* as an "independent science,"[21] *sui generis*, whose subject matter is human social organization. He called his science *ilm al-umran*.[22] Ibn Khaldun added:

> It also has its own peculiar problems — that is explaining the conditions that attach themselves to the essence of civilization, one after the other. Thus, the situation is the same with

this science as it is with any other science, whether it be a conventional or an intellectual one.

   It should be known that the discussion of this topic is something new, extraordinary, and highly useful. Penetrating research has shown the way to it.[23]

The science of *umran* is different from other sciences. It is for example, not politics, because politics is concerned with administering state or city in accordance with certain requirements, to direct the masses toward a behavior that will result in their preservation.[24] In a way, *ilm al-umran* "is an entirely original science. In fact, I have not come across a discussion along these lines by anyone."[25] Ibn Khaldun believed that he was inspired by God who led him "to a science" whose truth he ruthlessly set forth.

   If I have succeeded in presenting the problem of this science exhaustively and in showing how it differs in its various aspects and characteristics from all other crafts, this is due to divine guidance. If, on the other hand, I have omitted some point, or if the problems of this science have got confused with something else, the task of correcting remains for the discerning critic, but the merit is mine since I cleared and marked the way.[26]

This viewpoint was also emphasized on the last page of his *Muqaddimah*. In his "concluding remark," he stated that perhaps some other later scholars with "a solid scholarship, will penetrate into these problems in greater detail" than he did. He added:

   A person who creates a new discipline does not have the task of enumerating all the individual problems connected with it. His task is to specify the subject of the discipline and its various branches and the discussions connected with it. His ancestors, then, may gradually add more problems, until the discipline is completely presented.[27]

Ibn Khaldun specified the various branches or areas of his new science. They fall "naturally under six chapter headings," which he arranged "in an orderly way:"[28]

1. on human civilization in general, its various kinds, and the portion of the earth that is civilized;

2. on desert civilization, including a report on the tribes and savage nations;

3. on dynasties, the caliphate, and royal authority, including a discussion of government ranks;

4. on sedentary civilization, countries, and cities.

5. on crafts, ways of making a living, gainful occupations, and their various aspects; and

6. on the sciences, their acquisitions, and study.

Using present sociological terminology, Chapter 1 deals with human or social ecology; Chapter 2, with rural sociology, especially because Ibn Khaldun included ruralites under this heading; Chapter 3 with political sociology; Chapter 4, with urban sociology; and Chapter 5, to an extent, with economic sociology, including occupations and professions.

Because of the variety of topics with which this new science of social organization deals, it is, in one way or another, related to other social sciences.[29] However, historians "neglected the importance of change over the generations,"[30] including changes in customs and sectarian beliefs. As a result of its emphasis on the causes of change and variation within religious and other social groups, *The Muqaddimah* "has become unique, as it contains unusual knowledge."[31] The *Muqaddimah* is also unique for its emphasis on verifiable information. As will soon be seen, the goal of *ilm al-umran* is to formulate accurate laws of society and social change.[32] These laws, while not as rigid as those of natural sciences, "are sufficiently constant to cause social events to follow regular, well-defined patterns and sequences."[33] Such laws "operate on masses" and cannot be significantly influenced by isolated individual cases.[34] "When Ibn Khaldun speaks of science (*ilm*), he does not mean knowledge in the rough, but that certain and systematized knowledge which is science – not *Wissen*, but *Wissenschaft*."[35]

Methods

Applying the major characteristics of science to Ibn Khaldun's *ilm al-umran*, his science is:

1. *Theoretical*: Throughout *The Muqaddimah* several sociological generalizations are present. Ibn Khaldun laid much greater stress than most Muslim thinkers upon the inevitable working of cause and effect. What is important to his systematic procedure is that no polarization of cause or effect could be found.[36] He did not appeal to God as an explanatory principle underlying the whole of history.[37]

2. *Empirical*: To avoid speculation, one must rely on adequate methods to arrive at accurate generalizations. For this reason, Ibn Khaldun used the following methods:

a. *Observation*: According to Ibn Khaldun, part of the data "is direct information based upon personal observation."[38] Personal observation is an essential method for acquiring knowledge.[39]

Ibn Khaldun's wide experience as a diplomat, traveller, and writer, his participant observation of the nomadic life, and his firsthand knowledge of urban life have contributed to his emphasis on the significance of direct observation.[40] Here and there in *The Muqaddimah*, he specifically referred to his observation of social events.[41] Confident of his accurate observation, he occasionally remarked about his works: "Upon careful examination this will be found to be correct"[42] and "confirmed by direct observation."[43]

Some writers believe that Ibn Khaldun's field of observation was limited to the Arabs and Berbers of North Africa, and that his generalizations cannot be applied to other peoples of the world.[44] Nour also talks about "the elements of 'Islamic provincialism' "[45] in Ibn Khaldun's thinking. First, Ibn Khaldun's data were not limited to the Arabs and Berbers of North Africa. Such data encompassed the Syrians, the Persians, the Greeks, the Romans, the Turks, and others.[46] Second, Ibn Khaldun's data extended to non-Islamic peoples, such as the Jews, the Christians, and the Zorostrians.[47] Ibn Khaldun, especially in his *Ibar* used information from several diverse sources, *e.g.*, Muslim, Christian, and Jewish.[48] As Fischel points out, Ibn Khaldun did not follow his sources uncritically; he prudently and carefully verified their statements. He was particularly attuned to the cultural and religious manifestations and highlights of the history of non-Islamic peoples.[49] Thus, Nour's statement that

Ibn Khaldun "makes no sociological use of his own observations of the customs of the Christian Kingdom in Spain"[50] cannot be accepted. Ibn Khaldun, for example, discussed the customs of sedentary culture that "became firmly rooted in Spain."[51] He also showed how much of this specific sedentary culture was diffused to North Africa.[52] Third, even if Ibn Khaldun's generalizations are not applicable beyond North Africa, then this is not unique in social science. Some sociological studies are confined to one small community, one university, or one religious denomination.

b. *Comparison*: Ibn Khaldun used the comparative method in a variety of ways, mainly: (i) to compare dynasties before and during his time; (ii) to compare the dynasties of his time with each other; (iii) to compare a dynasty's life span with that of an individual's; (iv) to compare primitive bedouin society with civilized urban society; and (v) to compare his own data with those of other writers.

Ibn Khaldun believed that this method helps to clarify data; but he warned that it is "not safe from error." Together with forgetfulness and negligence, it sways the individual from his purpose and diverts him from his goal.[53] If a person has learned a good deal of a past history but remains unaware of the changes that conditions have undergone, he should not measure the historical information by the things he has observed with his own eyes, for the difference between the two is great.[54] Moreover, a person should not reject data for which he finds no observable parallels in his time. The world's conditions are not always the same.[55]

c. *Historical Method*: For his work, Ibn Khaldun collected data related to the origin, development, and growth of dynasties. He went further than historians of his time by showing the impact of such dynasties upon social relationships. He insisted that historical data must be carefully examined. "Little effort is being made to get at the truth . . . . Errors and unfounded assumptions are closely allied and familiar elements in historical information."[56] Some writers tend to exaggerate certain information without distinguishing between the nature of the possible and the impossible. Only those things within the sphere of the impossible should be accepted. Therefore, in discussing a given event, writers should not report the historical information about it mechanically. "It takes critical insight to sort out the hidden truth."[57]

Specific shortcomings that result from gathering historical information are as follows:[58]

i. Bias and partisanship in favor of a certain sect of school of thought. Prejudice and partisanship preclude critical investigation, and as a result, falsehood is accepted and transmitted.

ii. Reliance on false transmitters.

iii. Unawareness of the purpose of information. Unless an investigator is fully aware of an actor's goal, he is unable to understand the real meaning of his act.

iv. The tendency to believe, which often comes as a result of an unwarranted confidence in the transmitters of information. The numerousness of the reporters or transmitters does not necessarily indicate the indubitability or accuracy of the information.

v. Ignorance of the nature of the conditions arising in civilization and of the way these conditions conform with reality. Such conditions may be "affected by ambiguities and artificial distortions." Informants may not even be aware of them.

vi. Flattery and encomiums, which are used to approach men of power or rulers. Accordingly, false reports or information concerning these rulers may result. People naturally like to be praised and flattered and may encourage such false information to spread even if they do not really deserve it.

Ibn Khaldun then discussed the nature of the information with which historians usually deal. He differentiated "religious information" from that which deals with "actual events."[59] A person who studies religious information may not need to know social laws or "the nature of things which are born of civilization," for the divine revelation is the only source of religious information. Therefore, such information must be taken as it is, with no manipulation or alteration. The only thing one can do is to examine the integrity and truthfulness of the bearers of religious information.

From the preceding discussion, one may conclude that despite the fact that Ibn Khaldun was under the great impact of the traditionalism, which characterized his society, he clearly demonstrated his detached attitude and empirical method.[60]

3. *Cumulative:* Because human society undergoes changes over the generations, data and information may have to be extended or refined.[61]

According to Ibn Khaldun, "the easiest method of acquiring the scientific habit is through acquiring the ability to express oneself clearly in discussing and disputing scientific problems."[62] If a scholar finds an error in writings of other scholars, even if they are well known for their contributions, he should indicate his objection in writing so that future students of knowledge may know the difference.[63] Even if a discipline as a whole is incomplete and suffers shortcomings, scholars are duty-bound to correct such "problems — leaving no room for deficiency in it."[64] Scholars also should expose those guilty of plagiarism and deception.

> For instance, someone may try to ascribe the work of an earlier author to himself with the aid of certain tricks, such as changing the wording and the arrangement of the contents. Or, someone may eliminate material essential to a particular discipline, or mention unnecessary material, or replace correct statements with wrong ones, or mention useless material. All this shows ignorance and impudence.[65]

Thus, a critical investigation of information is essential in order to see whether the reported facts could have possibly happened.[66] The normative method for distinguishing right from wrong (by means of systematic or logical demonstration that admits of no doubts) "is to investigate human social organization."[67] In fact, this is the purpose of *The Muqaddimah*, to show that information about human social organization can be corrected, extended, and refined so that we can arrive at accurate theories.

Accordingly, the statement by Hussein that Ibn Khaldun did not examine the sources of his data,[68] is exaggerated. First, Ibn Khaldun examined, and when necessary corrected, the information he gathered. In his *Autobiography*, he pointed out that when he had finished writing *The Muqaddimah* and passed

on to other volumes of *al-Ibar*, he had a keen desire to construct
a number of books and collections that are only to be found in
great cities; and he had to correct and to make a fair copy.[69] Second, in many places in *The Muqaddimah*, Ibn Khaldun criticized scholars who do not examine information critically and
do not reject nonsensical stories about human social organization. Specifically, he criticized some of the writings of "thorough
scholars," such as al-Tabari, Ibn Rushd (Averroes), al-Turtooshi,
and al-Mas'udi.[70] Although al-Mas'udi impressed Ibn Khaldun
with a new method and outlook that influenced him in for-
mulating his own concepts of history, Ibn Khaldun, nevertheless, criticized him for having incorporated (into his
writings) stories and fables that have no basis in reality.[71]

4. *Nonethical (objective)*: The task of science is to study
social phenomena as they are. Ibn Khaldun explained social
events objectively and dispassionately.[72]

Several books describing what *ought to be*, not what *is*, were
published during Islam's history. Some orthodox writers indulged
in various utopias. They paid so much attention to the past and
the future that they missed the present. One of these books, *al-
Madina al-Fadilah (The Virtuous City)*, deserves special mention
here. It was written by al-Farabi, one of the well-known
Islamic philosophers (d. 950 A.D.). Plato's *Republic* probably
inspired al-Farabi's attempt to describe an ideal city-state.[73] He
seems to have keenly observed city life for the sole purpose of
condemning it.[74] Unlike al-Farabi, Ibn Khaldun seriously and
realistically analyzed city life in order to understand it and
adapt to it.

Mahdi believes that although Ibn Khaldun explained actual
events "with an extraordinary restraint and objectivity," and to
that extent he "resembles many a modern thinker," he, nevertheless, "was not an empiricist."[75] It should be noted that: a. the
nature and scope of empirical work is not the same in every
science — indeed, it varies from one science to another;
b. generally, empirical activities in social sciences are not as
rigorous as those of physical sciences; and c. some social scientists including some sociologists believe that any research activities based on careful observation or leading to accurate
knowledge can be called "empirical." The same is true in

philosophy, which defines the term empirical as "relating to experience; having reference to actual life," and defines "empiricism" as "a proposition about the sources of knowledge . . . about origins of ideas, concepts, or universal . . . practice, method, or methodology; relying upon direct observation or immediate experience."[76] As Durkheim stated, empirical knowledge "is that which is brought into our minds by the direct actions of objects."[77]

Bouthoul also believed that Ibn Khaldun's objectivity was narrow, which led him to accept everything,[78] including the belief in the jinn.[79] First of all, Ibn Khaldun stated clearly that stories about jinn "intended to indicate ugliness and frightfulness"; they are "not meant to be taken literally," for they are "made up of nonsensical elements which are absurd for various reasons."[80] Second, Bouthoul's statement contradicts, to some extent, some statements he made in his same work dealing with Ibn Khaldun's emphasis on observation.[81]

A question was also raised as to whether Ibn Khaldun's religious belief had a great influence upon his scientific endeavors. Ibn Khaldun was a devout Muslim, but he did not explain *ilm al-umran* in theological terms. He used *The Koran* as *a* source of information; and the different Koranic verse with which he ended each chapter may be thought of purely as a ritual aside.[82] It was a customary way of writing at his time.

II. Ibn Khaldun and Comte: Convergencies and Divergencies

Despite their divergent ideas, Ibn Khaldun and Comte converged in their scientific methodology and in some other important aspects of their writings.

1. Each believed that his own work was something new;[83] Ibn Khaldun called it *ilm al-umran* (science of human social organization), and Comte named it *sociology*. The subject matter of these alike sciences is human society. Ibn Khaldun repeatedly emphasized that his science is independent, *sui generis*.

2. The objective of Comte's sociology was to improve human society. He was, along with other social thinkers such as

Marx and Spencer, concerned with the impact of industrialism upon political, economic, and intellectual life, especially in Europe. More than others, Comte is labelled by some writers as an idealist in his thinking about the future development of human society. Ibn Khaldun, conversely, was interested in describing human society rather than discovering any remedy for its ills, although he can be considered a conciliator of nomadism and Islam.[84] Although Ibn Khaldun was more realistic than Comte, to declare that the Arab thinker was entirely lacking in idealism is an exaggeration.[85] One can detect in Ibn Khaldun's writings his concern for the rise and decline of states in his time. By sending copies of *The Muqaddimah* to the heads of the North African states, perhaps Ibn Khaldun indirectly was expressing his wish to see a strong and stable state.

3. Comte sought society's emancipation from theological and metaphysical conceptions by emphasizing a positivistic or scientific stage of development. Ibn Khaldun detached his work from metaphysical influence and emphasized objective and reliable information.

4. Both attempted to discover laws of social life that are analogous to natural laws, by which social phenomena can be understood and explained. Durkheim clearly acknowledged Comte's contribution in this regard and suggested further that the sociologist "put himself in the same state of mind as the physicist, chemist, or physiologist."[86]

5. Hence, by emphasizing verifiable knowledge, each *ilm al-umran* and sociology is a predictive discipline.

6. Ibn Khaldun and Comte utilized observation, comparison, and historical data as research methods. Ibn Khaldun began as a historian, and is considered the founder of a scientific history.[87] Comte emphasized historical method in his writing; and for a long time, the historical method was to be the method of sociology, although he himself acknowledged the difficulty of applying it "on account of the extreme complexity of the materials we have to deal with."[88]

7. Neither Comte nor Ibn Khaldun used quantitative techniques of research. Neither "sociology nor *ilm al-umran* was identified or associated with the use of statistics and mathematics. The Belgian statistician Adolphe Quetelet (1796–1874)

might be considered the first to attempt linking statistics, as a research tool, with social behavior. Comte and Ibn Khaldun were concerned with observation. The latter's rigorous demand that the method of observation be used comprehensively and with accuracy led some modern thinkers to generalize that "the logico-observational character of his work is striking throughout."[89]

8. Both distinguished their sciences, *sociology* and *ilm al-umran*, respectively, from other related disciplines. Comte's sociology is not politics, economics, or jurisprudence, but something different. Ibn Khaldun's *ilm al-umran* "has its own peculiar object," which is not politics, rhetoric, philosophy, or history.

9. Comte did not single out any specific social unit for analysis because he believed that the whole (human society) is better known than its parts.[90] For Ibn Khaldun, however, *badawa* (nomadism-ruralism) and *hadara* (urbanism) in relation to the rise and decline of states might be considered units for analysis.

10. Both believed that the human nature is basically the same everywhere.

11. Both opposed individualism.

12. Comte stated that people are not equal. Generally, this statement is similar to Ibn Khaldun's discussion of specialization, occupations, and professions. The latter stated that "differences of condition among people are the result of the different ways in which they make their livings."[91]

13. Comte was explicit and more specific about his division of society into two major parts: statics and dynamics. Such a division was used implicitly by Ibn Khaldun in his discussion of the conflict between nomadism and urbanism.

14. Both recognized the importance of social change and were concerned with the actual change, each in his own society. Ibn Khaldun was specifically critical of writers who neglected change as a significant aspect of social life.

15. The premise of Comte's theory, "the faith in evolution toward progress," was faulty;[92] the premise of Ibn Khaldun's theory, the constant rise and fall of states, also, to a great extent, was faulty. (See Chapter 6.)

The contributions of the two men are many, especially to a new vocabulary for the new science. According to Schmidt, Comte's definition and methods of "sociology" should not be regarded as final. Schmidt and Gumplowicz maintained that the discipline existed long before the time of Comte, and that Ibn Khaldun, in particular, anticipated certain conclusions that seemed to him of fundamental significance.[93]

Now a daring question may be raised: *Was Comte familiar with Ibn Khaldun's writings?*

It seems that Ibn Khaldun's name appeared in Europe for the first time in 1636, when Jacob Golius published in Leiden the work of Ibn Arabshah *Aja'ib al-Makdoor fi Akhbar Timur*.[94] In 1697, a biography of Ibn Khaldun appeared in *D'Herbelot's Bibliotheque Orientale*. In 1806 and in 1810, Sylvester de Sacy published his translation of segments of Ibn Khaldun's *Muqaddimah* into French; and in 1816, he published "an ample description" of this book. About the same time, in 1812, von Hammer-Purgstall published a treatise "in which he particularly referred to some of Ibn Khaldun's theories on the decline of states, and described him as "the Montesquieu of the Arabs' ('ein arabische Montes-quieu')". Afterward,he published a German translation of some passages of *The Muqaddimah* in the *Journal Asiatique* (1822).[95] At the same time, de Sacy and some of his colleagues continued to publish translation of parts of *The Muqaddimah*. (The complete text of the book was translated and published later.)[96] Was Comte aware of the French segments of Ibn Khaldun's work? If he was not, would it not be unusual for a scholar like him in the scholarly atmosphere that he experienced not to be familair with such a published work? One may also assume that Ibn Khaldun's main ideas reached Comte through Comte's three Egyptian disciples, including Mazhar Beg.[97] Another assumption is that because Comte was, to some extent, influenced by Montesquieu, and that Montesquieu was familiar with some of Ibn Khaldun's writing,[98] Comte, therefore, might have been indirectly influenced by Ibn Khaldun. It should be noted that these are mere assumptions. Moreover, the obvious differences between Comte's sociology and Ibn Khaldun's *ilm al*-umran, both in scope and application, cannot be ignored.

Science is a cultural invention, a new combination of elements that already exist in the cultural base. Ibn Khaldun was quite aware of this cultural fact.[99] This might explain the reason for some writers to believe that "Comte made very few original contributions: almost all of his ideas can be traced back to numerous predecessors."[100] The same has also been said about Ibn Khaldun. Regardless of these comments, some writers still declare that Comte is the "father" of sociology; and others still maintain that Ibn Khaldun is the "founder" of this new science.[101] Even those who believe that Ibn Khaldun's "claim to originality appears somewhat exaggerated," emphasize, nevertheless, that he developed, as no one had done before, the science now called sociology.[102]

Chapter 3

SOCIETY, CULTURE, AND SOCIALIZATION

This chapter presents in some detail Ibn Khaldun's theoretical treatment of the concepts society, culture, socialization process, and social control. More emphasis is placed on his discussion of society as a reality, *sui generis*. The chapter also shows how Ibn Khaldun advocated social determinism and why he is considered a realist.

Ibn Khaldun studied human society, its structure, functions, processes, and changes; but he did not formally define the concept society. He is, in this respect, not alone among social scientists. Neither Comte, nor Spencer, nor Durkheim, nor Weber, nor Simmel formally defined society. To Comte, society is a collective organism, a harmony of structure and function, working toward a common goal. Spencer regarded society as a politically organized entity whose members arrange themselves in somewhat permanent forms; that is, society is an organism that maintains an equilibration. To Weber, society consists of a complex of meaningful human interrelationships. And Simmel's conception of society is, to some extent, similar to Weber's, although he preferred to speak not of society, but of socialization.[1] The system of relations Simmel referred to as moral, legal, and conventional is similar to Durkheim's view of societal morality: "It is not a simple juxtaposition of individuals who bring an intrinsic morality with them, but rather man is a moral being only because he lives in society . . . . Morality, in all its forms, is never met with except in society. It never varies except in relation to social conditions."[2]

I. Society: Sui Generis

Ibn Khaldun repeatedly emphasized human need for a social organization to guide them. He agreed with earlier philosophers that man is social by nature. For Ibn Khaldun, the individual cannot exist without social interaction. In order to obtain their livelihoods and other necessities, people cannot live and exist except through social organization and cooperation.[3] Human beings possess peculiar qualities that can distinguish them from other living beings: (1) the ability to think and hence to acquire sciences and crafts; (2) "the need for restraining influence and strong authority" that come to them through thinking not instincts; (3) the concerted efforts, including cooperation, to obtain their livelihoods by various ways and means; and (4) civilization, i.e., to settle together in towns and cities for the satisfaction of their needs, and for comforts and companionship.[4] These ideas are similar to those of Comte who emphatically stressed man's social tendencies and his need for company of his fellow human beings. They are also similar to Durkheim's idea that society is the source of all the higher values of civilization which raises him above the animal level.

Rosenthal states: "Gifted with shrewd insight into the world as it is, [Ibn Khaldun] constructed a theory of the origin, growth and development of human society."[5] Ibn Khaldun sought the formulation of the laws of human society. Specifically, he discussed the types of human society, the nomadic[6] and the sedentary, and pointed out the influence of political, economic, and geographic factors on the development of such societies.

Society for Ibn Khaldun, as for Durkheim, is that domain in which social phenomena occur. Both thinkers considered society itself a natural phenomenon subject to laws.[7] Unlike Ibn Khaldun, and for this matter unlike Durkheim, the classical economists believed that nothing is real in society except the individual.[8]

Thus, to Ibn Khaldun, society is a reality, *sui generis*. Similar to Durkheim's views, this reality is above and apart from the individual; that is, "the representations which express it have a wholly different contents from purely individual ones."[9] More explicit than Ibn Khaldun, Durkheim pointed out that the "substance of social life cannot be explained by purely psychological factors, *i.e.*, by the states of individual consciousness."[10] It can be generalized that Ibn Khaldun is the first thinker to make society the subject matter of a new independent science. He was able to study and analyze human society, divide it into scientifically utilizable categories, and develop from his data generalizations that have "a permanent interest and permanent value for that movement of thought known as sociology."[11]

Interestingly Ibn Khaldun differentiated between primary and secondary social relationships. Secondary relationships, are those of strangers, or "client relationships, and contacts with slaves or allies," but "a special closeness of relationship," can develop between master and followers, which "strengthens the close contact."[12] The primary relationships, on the other hand, are based on "the feeling of close contact . . . friendly association, long familiarity, and the companionship that results from growing up together . . . . If close contact is established in such a manner, the result will be affection and cooperation. Observation of people shows this to be so."[13] In modern sociology, the "primary group" concept, popularized by Charles H. Cooley, stresses the intimacy of face-to-face association. It is primary in several senses but chiefly in that it is "fundamental in forming the social nature and ideas of the individual."[14] The concept "secondary group" denotes a large number of individuals characterized by impersonal social contacts. Social relationships, whether primary or secondary, are to Ibn Khaldun as to Tönnies "willed" relationships, and are "purposive."[15] They are to Ibn Khaldun as to Simmel and Durkheim group oriented.

Features of Human Society

According to Ibn Khaldun, certain features are essential for the survival of human society.

1. Society as a whole, not the individual, is the important force for self-preservation against human and physical elements. This explains "the need of human beings for social organization and the impossibility of their living and existing by themselves."[16] Each individual needs the help of others for his defense. The duration of one's life is not only maintained by society's numerical strength, but also by its unity. Even if several groups exist, one is probably stronger than another or all the other groups combined. Society is the largest group within a territory.[17]

2. Human society needs a leader or a ruler. "The human species must have a person who will cause them to act in accordance with what is good for them and who will prevent them by force from doing things harmful to them."[18] Without a ruler disagreement may lead to "trouble" that, in turn, may lead to the destruction and uprooting of individuals.[19] If the leader's rule over people is based upon rational politics then "People are obliged to submit to it in view of the reward they expect from the ruler after he has become acquainted with what is good for them."[20] The leadership or the restraining influence need not be religious. "When Muslims agree upon the practice of justice and observance of the divine laws, no *imam* [religious leader] is needed, and the position of *imam* is not necessary."[21] As will be seen, leadership exists through superiority, which is caused by group solidarity (*asabiyah*).

3. Activities necessary for the welfare of human society are distributed among qualified persons. This is because, "by himself, the ruler is weak"; and "he must look for help from his fellow men."[22] These activities can be maintained through coordination, for this is the only way human beings can satisfy the need of a number many times greater than themselves.[23] Ibn Khaldun came very close to Comte's statement that the distribution of such activities is necessary for the growth of the state.[24] Durkheim contended that "although Comte recognized that the division of labor is a source of solidarity, it seems that he did not perceive that this solidarity is *sui generis* and is little by little substituted for that which social likenesses give rise to."[25] Durkheim, however, emphasized the same idea common to Ibn Khaldun and Comte; *i.e.*, "higher societies can maintain

themselves in equalibrium only if labor is divided."[26] Briefly, the division of social labor, as Ibn Khaldun, Durkheim, and Simmel maintained, is a form of differentiation in human society, a shift from homogeneity to heterogeneity.

4. Human society functions as a whole through cooperation. Because "human beings cannot live and exist except through social organization and cooperation,"[27] it is absolutely necessary for them to have the cooperation of their fellow men. This is reminiscent of Durkheim's work that "society cannot exist if its parts are not solidary."[28] In fact, discussion of the need for cooperation in human society has been advanced by many thinkers through the centuries. In Islam, Ikhwan al-Safa stressed the significance of cooperation for the survival of human society and for its continuous happiness. Several other Muslim thinkers, *e.g.*, al-Farabi and Ibn Sina (Avicenna), advocated the same idea.[29] And in classical sociology Spencer, for instance, who did not make the state coextensive with society, believed that society is supported by two types of cooperation, spontaneous private cooperation which does not affect the society as a unit except in indirect ways and the "consciously devised" cooperation which deals with the society as a whole.[30]

Cooperation is possible because, Ibn Khaldun emphasized, "man is more inclined toward good qualities than toward bad qualities."[31] It is, then, "in the nature of human beings to enter into close contact and to associate with each other even though they may not have a common descent."[32] Because cooperatoin is essential for the survival of human society, coercion may be used, especially if people are either largely ignorant of, or ignoring, the interests of other human beings.[33]

To Ibn Khaldun, society is not a haphazard entity. He perceived the interdependence of the religious, political, economic, military, and cultural spheres of human society. They are inseparable and linked with one another; a change in one sphere or aspect affects others in one way or another.[34] This conception of society as a system in equilibrium was reaffirmed by Durkheim and other sociologists. It is considered "Pareto's most important contribution to sociological theory."[35] In dealing with human society, Durkheim as well as Gumplowicz did not escape the language of biological functionalism, especially in their constant references to such terms as "ends," "purposes,"[36] and "functions."

Although Ibn Khaldun stressed the idea that "general consensus is the protection and defense"[37] for society, this does not mean that such a society is devoid of conflicts. Conflict does exist in human society because aggressiveness is natural to human beings. Aggressiveness and injustice cause dissension. "Dissension leads to hostilities, and hostilities lead to trouble and bloodshed and loss of life," which explains why "wars and different kinds of fighting have always occured in the world."[38]

Thus, society always involves cooperation and conflict, an idea advocated later in some detail by Simmel. Both Ibn Khaldun and Simmel felt that conflict is an essential part of social interaction. Becker and Barnes believed that these ideas of Ibn Khaldun place him among the conflict theorists.[39] Details of Ibn Khaldun's theoretical explanations of conflict will be discussed later.

5. Society has a common territory. "Each dynasty has a certain amount of provinces and lands, and no more."[40]. This is one way to distinguish people who establish society and support it from those who do not. It is also one way to protect the society against enemies. It is, further, one way to enforce within this territory the laws of the society relative to the restrictions, collection of taxes, and other requirements. If a society reaches "its farthest extension," i.e., expansion beyond its holdings, "its widening territory remains without military protection and is laid open to any chance attack by enemy or neighbor,"[41] especially if the members of that society lack a strong social solidarity.

6. Society forms culture. "Custom causes human nature to incline toward the thing to which it becomes used. Man is the child of customs."[42] Culture consists of the numerous things in the world, including written works. "They are handed down among all races [people] and in all ages. They differ as the result of differences in religious laws and organizations and in the information available about nations and dynasties."[43] Thus, culture is shared by the members of human society.

7. Sense of belongingness. Society usually persists for a long time if the social solidarity (asabiyah) or sense of belongingness to the society is strong. Asabiyah, then, determines the

durability of human society. The stronger the *asabiyah*, the more likely that society is to persist.

Aggresiveness and defensive strength, obtained through *asabiyah*, lead to mutual affection and "willingness to fight and die for each other."[44] However, people whose *asabiyah* "cannot defend them against oppression certainly cannot offer any opposition or press any claim. They have submitted to humble meekness."[45] In this regard, *asabiyah* as a psychological factor and a driving force in the development of human society may, to some extent, be equated to nationalism.[46] The concept of *asabiyah* will be discussed later. (See Chapter 4.)

II. Culture

Culture, according to Tylor, is a complex whole that includes all forms of knowledge, beliefs, art, laws, customs, and any other capabilities acquired by people as members of society.[47] Culture is, then, a product of human society, an idea emphasized by Ibn Khaldun.

People, according to Ibn Khaldun, are distinguished from animals by their ability to think and thus to establish social organizations and culture.[48] Culture, Ibn Khaldun reiterated, "does not happen haphazardly."[49] Cultural aspects, especially written works, are handed down among all people in all ages.[50] Moreover, culture can make actions "orderly and not likely to be detrimental."[51] This is because culture is learned.[52] People "acquire the manner needed in dealing with human beings"[53] from their parents, teachers, and others. A violation of such manners or norms can bring ridicule or any type of social pressure. This is because customs are "like a second nature." A person who, for instance, has seen his father and older men wear certain clothes, will not be able to diverge from or "brusque disregard" of his forebears' customs in this respect. Were he to do it, he would be accused of insanity.[54]

Culture Change

Culture, according to Ibn Khaldun, is a way of life that may "change with a change of periods and the passing of days . . . . The condition of the world and of nations, their customs and sects, does not persist in the same form or in a constant manner."[55] A declining dynasty may bring about changes in social customs, because the customs of each people depend on the customs of its ruler. When politically ambitious men seize power, "they inevitably have recourse to the customs of their predecessors and adopt most of them."[56]

Political, economic, and religious factors affecting change will be discussed in other chapters. Here, the importance of geographic factors is briefly presented.

The conditioning role of geographical factors in their relation to human society has been mentioned by many thinkers before and after Ibn Khaldun, including several medieval men such as Giovanni Villani, St. Thomas Aquinas, Michelangello, Machiavelli, and Jean Bodin.[57] Ibn Khaldun's analysis of the influence of physical environment upon social organization is considered more thorough than that of other studies of the subject "until the time of Bodin, if not until that of Montesquieu."[58]

Geographic factors affect color and character qualities of the human beings. Ibn Khaldun disagreed with genealogists and others who imagined that the blacks "are the children of Ham, the son of Noah, and that they were singled out to be black as the result of Noah's curse, which produced Ham's color."[59] The following explains Ibn Khaldun's geographic determinism:

> It is mentioned in the Torah [Gen. 9:25] that Noah cursed his son Ham. No reference is made there to blackness. The curse included no more than that Ham's descendents should be the slaves of his brother's descendents. To attribute the blackness of the Negroes to Ham, reveals disregard of the true nature of heat and cold and of the influence they exercise upon the air (climate) and upon the creatures that come into being in it. The black color (of skin) common to the inhabitants of the first and second zones is the result of the composition of the air in which they live, and which comes about under the influence of the greatly increased heat in the south. The sun is at the zenith there twice a year at short intervals. In almost all seasons, the sun is in culmination for a long time. The light of the sun, therefore, is plentiful. People there have to undergo a very severe summer. Something similar happens in the two corresponding zones to the north, the seventh and sixth zones.

There, a white color (of skin) is common among the inhabitants, likewise the result of the composition of the air in which they live, and which comes about under the influence of the excessive cold in the north. The sun is always on the horizon within the visual field of the human observer, or close to it. It never ascends to the zenith, nor even gets close to it. The heat, therefore, is weak in the region, and the cold severe in almost all seasons. In consequence, the color of the inhabitants is white, and they tend to have little body hair. Further consequences of the excessive cold are blue eyes, freckled skin, and blond hair.[60]

Ibn Khaldun, further, emphasized his point: Blacks from the south who settle in the temperate zone or in the cold zone "are found to produce descendants whose color gradually turns white in the course of time." Vice versa, inhabitants from the north or from the temperate zone who settle in the south produce descendants whose color turns black.[61]

During Ibn Khaldun's time, many people believed that the blacks "are in general characterized by levity, excitability, and great emotionalism," and that "they are found eager to dance whenever they hear a melody."[62] Ibn Khaldun, however, clearly attributed the development of these characteristics to geographical factors. He criticized those scholars, *e.g.*, Galen, who believed "that the reason is a weakness of their [the blacks'] brains which results in a weakness of their intellect."[63] Ibn Khaldun insisted that "this is an inconclusive and unproven statement."[64]

III. Socialization Process

Besides the explanation of the mental ability of the blacks, Ibn Khaldun offered a sociocultural interpretation for the question of intelligence of other groups. For example, he discussed the belief current in his time that "Eastern people" were more intelligent and scientifically minded than "Western inhabitants," *e.g.*, North Africans. He firmly declared that this is not because of any difference in the original constitution of mind, as misinformed travelers tended to believe.[65] All men, Western and

Eastern, are about the same in their mental potential; the difference arises only as a result of differing cultures and social
development. Mind is largely a product of the social environment; that is, knowledge increases or decreases only because of
the contacts and experience the person receives from his sur-
roundings. Some nomads are originally more intelligent than
many of the urbanites; but urbanization and its concomitants,
for example crafts and refined technical habits and manners
associated with urban conditions, make urbanites appear more
sophisticated than nomads.[66]

Knowledge is acquired.[67] By nature, human beings are
ignorant; but because of their ability to think, they learn by
acquiring knowledge and technique.[68] Even the ability for
sorcery requires exercise "in order to be capable of transformation from potentiality into actuality"; hence, it is a learning process.[69]

A person's isolation from human contact limits his observation, experience, and knowledge about the world in which he
lives. Ibn Khaldun told an instructive story of a boy who was
imprisoned with his father from his early infancy and,
therefore, was unable to imagine or understand correctly what
his father told him about the outside world. He could not correctly think of things that were beyond his familiar
experience.[70]

Socialization, then, is defined by Ibn Khaldun as a process
by which "human beings obtain their knowledge and character
qualities and all their opinions and virtues" through study, imitation, personal contact, and travel.[71] One's knowledge of things
is limited. One's "whole lifetime would not suffice to know all
the literature that exists in a single discipline, even if he were
to devote himself entirely to it."[72] The individual who has gained
experience of a particular craft " is rarely able afterward to
master another."[73]

Ibn Khaldun stressed the fact that the socialization process
begins after birth. At birth, the individual "has no knowledge
whatever."[74] That is, the human mind is blank, *tabula rasa*. "In
his first condition, before he has attained discernment, man is
simply matter, in as much as he is ignorant of all knowledge. He
reaches perfection of his form through knowledge, which he

acquires through his own organs."[75] In the family, the individual acquires the habits and other forms of behavior from his parents. It is there that the child "is able" to distinguish between vice and virtue in his actions on the basis of his expectation of punishment and reward.[76] "Children constantly imitate their fathers. They do that only because they see perfection in them."[77] The family also is a circle for affection. "Compassion and affection for one's blood relations and relatives exist in human nature."[78] The family is characterized by "mutual support and aid."[79] "Those who have no one of their own lineage to care for rarely feel affection for their fellows."[80]

It is in the family that the individual acquires his religion. Ibn Khaldun quoted Muhammad: "Every infant is born in the natural state. It is his parents who make him a Jew or a Christian or a Magian."[81] Religion is not only a form of social control; religious ideals themselves are "capable of inspiring man to create permanent values which survive dynastic and national-political boundaries."[82]

Teachers and elders are also important agents in the process of socialization. The individual acquires from them "the manners needed in dealing with human beings." These "manners" include the habits, customs, traditions, language, music, and religious interpretations. This is equivalent to formal education. Ibn Khaldun asserted that "scientific instruction is a craft."[83] Because the human mind is capable of acquiring knowledge, "the right attitude in scientific instruction and toward the method of giving such instruction" must be stressed. Accordingly, knowledge may have to be obtained "gradually and little by little,"[84] inasmuch as the person's preparedness keeps growing gradually until he has a comprehensive knowledge of the problems of the discipine he studies. However, some teachers are "ignorant" of this "effective method of instruction." They begin their instruction by confronting the student with obscure scientific problems and require him to concentrate on solving them. "They think that that is experienced and correct teaching, and they make it the task of the student to comprehend and know such things." In actuality, "they merely confuse him by exposing him to the final results of a discipline at the beginning of his studies." This is a "poor instruction, and nothing else," because the confused student "becomes indolent. He stops thinking. He despairs of becoming a scholar and avoids scholarship and instruction."[85] A formal learning process, moreover, should be void of memorization. "Memorization leads to forgetfulness."[86]

Ibn Khaldun was convinced that people are the prime movers of the socialization process. If they are willing to learn then this process would be easily accomplished. Conversely, if they are not willing to acquire knowledge they usually need longer time for this purpose.[87]

Language is another essential factor for socialization. Ibn Khaldun provided the following example. An Arab child who is reared among nomadic people usually learns their language and has a good knowledge of the vowel endings and of eloquent Arabic expression. "But he does not have any knowledge whatever of grammatical rules. His correctness and eloquence of speech is purely the result of the linguistic habit he has obtained."[88] Through language, people are able to express their intentions, "because by their very nature cooperation and social organization are made easier by proper expressions."[89] Much of human social contacts are based on communications that "take place through 'verbal expression.'" Written communication is also utilized by people. "Each nation has its own particular form of writing."[90] Language, thus, is symbolic. "Linguistic expression is merely the interpreter of ideas that are in the mind."[91] Acquiring these aspects of culture at an early age makes them "firmly established."[92] This includes "improper language" which is used by many people in the presence of their friends, superiors, and womenfolk. "They are not deterred by any sense of restraint, because the bad custom of behaving openly in an improper manner in both words and deeds has taken hold of them."[93]

Ibn Khaldun further believed that music is another form of expression of human behavior. Listening to music and sounds leads to pleasure and emotion, "a kind of drunkenness," which causes the individual "to make light of difficulties," especially if the "sounds are harmonious." This is why music and poetical songs are used during war to stir the fighters to meet their rivals. People have learned to do this through experience.[94] These ideas are similar to those of Ikhwan al-Safa.[95]

Ibn Khaldun's major ideas of the socialization process can be summed up in this quotation from his *Muqaddimah*:

> Man is a child of the customs and the things he has become used to. He is not the product of his natural disposition and temperament. The conditions to which he has become accustomed, until they have become for him a quality of character and matters of habit and custom, have replaced his natural disposition. If one studies this in human beings, one will find much of it, and it will be found to be a correct observation.[96]

As will be seen, Ibn Khaldun used this observation to apply the principle of cause and effect to the nomads. The nomads, as a result of their peculiar life in the desert, cannot be different from what they are. The tribe that roams the desert, under no rule but the rule of the sword, must be rough, or it will sooner or later perish. It is, moreover, this socialization process that made and still makes the nomadic man disposed toward poetry rather than toward science. Scientific discipline requires a more or less calm disposition to which the nomadic man is ordinarily unaccustomed. The constant raiding and fighting of desert life have made him a man of emotion and quick anger.

Sociologists from Comte to present time have stressed the significance of social environment. Comte stated that people cannot emancipate themselves from the environment's influence.[97] Durkheim emphasized that the individual cannot be a social being without acquiring cultural habits or symbols from others.[98] Simmel went further by defining sociology as "the study of the forms of socializations." Cooley's "looking-glass self" and Mead's "generalized others" are perhaps the most widely cited theoretical concepts in the sociopsychological literature. Briefly stated, according to Cooley, the "self" is usually a product of social environment. People see themselves as they think others see them.[99] Mead's concept, the "generalized others," indicates the impression people have of society's expectations. When man thinks, he merely converses with those "others."[100] As Mills stated, "it is from this socially constituted viewpoint that one approves or disapproves of given arguments as logical or illogical, valid or invalid."[101]

IV. Social Control

Like the eighteenth century English Deists, Ibn Khaldun seemd to believe that after creating the world God left it to be run by its own laws without intervention. Even the prophets who are sent by God tend to achieve their sacred missions according to social laws. They do not attempt to change the traditions and mores of society.[102] For Ibn Khaldun, religion is *a* means of social control, *i.e.*, social control is not always a result of religion. He pointed out that "existence and human life can materialize without the existence of prophecy";[103] that people manage, nevertheless, to live in well-organized societies. Human society is an independent entity and can be treated apart from religious laws, whose "restraining influence is something inherent."[104]

Ibn Khaldun believed that man is more inclined toward goodness or good qualities than toward bad qualities.[105] Indeed, "evil qualities" in man such as injustice and aggression exist; but, unlike animals, human beings seek restraining influence and strong authority, without which they cannot survive.[106] Therefore, their need for social organization is indispensable. In every group, having an accepted authority in order to prevent people from attacking each other is necessary. The religious institution, necessary to human beings, has a better understanding of the public interests.[107] It "causes rudeness and pride to disappear" and exercises a restraining influence on people's envy and jealousy.[108] Ibn Khaldun's ideas here are similar to those of Comte, Durkheim, and several social scientists, that religion as a social institution is one of the most significant regulative agencies in society.[109]

To Ibn Khaldun, then, social control is of two types: religious and political. In addition to religious laws, "it is necessary to have reference to ordained political norms, which are accepted by the mass and to whose laws it submits."[110] Societal "laws have their reasons in the purposes they are to serve," whether this is related to adultery, murder, or any injustice that might hamper preservation of social organization.[111] For example, it sould not be objected that punishment for highway robbery is provided for in the law, because this action is considered an injustice that can be committed by someone who has the ability not only to commit it, but also to cause fear. This fear enables him to take away the property of others.[112]

Ibn Khaldun explained the fact that injustice is of many kinds. Injustice does not imply only the confiscation of money or other property from the owners without compensation. It is more than that. Whoever takes away someone's property, "or uses him for forced labor, or presses an unjustified claim against him, or imposes upon him a duty not required by the religious law, does an injustice to that particular person." Those who collect unjustified taxes or infringe upon property rights or deny people their rights commit an injustice. Society suffers from all these acts, especially when people have lost all incentive.[113]

Ibn Khaldun believed that to punish criminals, fines are not sufficient by themselves. Payment of fines "is often an incentive" rather than a deterrent to crime, especially if the crime is a serious one. This situation could lead to social disorganization and anarchy.[114]

Ibn Khaldun realized that deviance from rules may be committed by men of power themselves. As he stated:

> Injustice can be committed only by persons who cannot be touched, only by persons who have power and authority. Therefore, injustice has been very much censured, and repeated threats against it have been expressed in the hope that perhaps the persons who are able to commit injustice will find a restraining influence in themselves.[115]

Chapter 4

ASABIYAH
(SOCIAL SOLIDARITY)

As one of the most important concepts in Ibn Khaldun's writings, *asabiyah (esprit de corps* or social solidarity) is seen here as the seed of the Khaldunian cyclical theory of human history. The major characteristics of *asabiyah* and its role in developing a new state are presented. The next two chapters give a detailed explanation of the cyclical movement.

Asabiyah, as one of the most significant concepts in Ibn Khaldun's work and as the most important factor in the development of society, is derived from the Arabic root *asab* (to bind), *i.e.,* to bind the individuals into a group (*asabtun, usbatun,* or *isabatun*). *Asabiyah* is also a form derived from *asaba,* which designates the concept that is etymologically abstracted from the concrete form.[1] What Ibn Khaldun specifically meant by the term *asabiyah* is difficult to decide. In spite of his great reliance upon this term, he never clearly defined it. The term seems to have been quite familiar or known in his time; thus, he did not feel a need to define it. The term *asabiyah* has been translated as "esprit de corps," "partisanship," "famille," "parti," "tribal consciousness," "blood relationship," "tribal spirit," "tribal loyalty," "vitality," "feeling of unity," "group adhesion," "groupdom," "sense of solidarity," "group mind," "collective consciousness," "group feeling," "group solidarity," "feeling of solidarity," and "social solidarity." De Slane's French translation, *esprit de corps*, and the English translation, "social solidarity," seem to be closest to the original term.

Simon believes that the terms *asabiyah* and solidarity do not mean exactly the same. One of the reasons for this divergence is that " 'solidarity' is on a higher level of abstraction than *asabiyah*. (There is no plural form of the word solidarity, but this is not so with *asabiyah*)." *Asabiyah* is the reflection of a concrete group cohesion, not of cohesion in general. Accordingly, Simmon suggests keeping the Arabic term, because ultimately it cannot be translated adequately.[2] In his translation of segments from *The Muqaddimah*, Schimmel kept the term *asabiyah* untranslated.[3] Indeed, keeping the Arabic term is appropriate not only because it cannot be accurately translated, but also because the term has very seldom if ever been used in modern or contemporary Arabic literature. Interest in the term is not as such but in knowing how Ibn Khaldun himself used it. *Asabiyah* in the doctrine of Ibn Khaldun means the sense of social solidarity; hence, *social* when it is applied to a social group or people who live in a given space or community and have a lifestyle they endeavor to maintain.

Asabiyah, then, is a social bond that can be used to measure the strength and stability of social groupings. This abstract concept conveys the idea of the bond that ensures the cohesion of a social group just as, analogously, the tendons ensure the cohesion of flesh to the bones.[4] However, this bond, *asabiyah*, is not necessarily based on consanguinal relation. It is a social as well as psychological, physical, and political phenomenon, manifesting itself most clearly among, but not confined to, the nomadic or tribal people.

Asabiyah is identical with Durkheim's *collective conscience*. Ibn Khaldun emphasized that in *asabiyah* the individual's descent, birth, and even identity are normally "lost" to, or fused into, the group of which he is a member; "he thus becomes one of the others."[5] Such a group thinks and behaves as a unit. Personality is only a function of the social structure. Even if an individual group has as many diverse *asabiyahs* still an *asabiyah* must exist that is stronger than all the others combined, which is capable of making them coalesce and subservient. Without such a unity, dissension and strife occur.[6] Such a united *asabiyah* produces the ability to protect and defend oneself and when necessary to press one's claim.[7] People whose *asabiyah* is strong do not usually fear oppression or aggression. Briefly, then, it suffices to state that this group spirit or unity, *asabiyah*, makes the individual devote himself to his group and view the world through its eyes. It is, as Hitti stated, " the individualism of the member of the clan magnified."[8]

Durkheim, conversely, believed that "the more primitive societies are, the more resemblances there are among individuals who compose them."[9] A society of this type is more or less an "organized totality of beliefs and sentiments common to all members of the group."[10] Such a solidarity is *sui generis* that links the person with society.[11] Consequently, a collective conscience becomes "a source of life,"[12] which is to be defended "against all enemies within and without."[13] Moreover, "the nature of collective sentiments accounts for punishment, and consequently, for crime." A crime is an act contrary to "strong and defined states of the common conscience."[14] The reaction to crime is general and collective; it comes from society which considers crime an "attack directed against it" – against the common conscience, which ought to resist it and repress it by punishment.[15]

In a broader perspective, Ibn Khaldun's discussion of *asabiyah* is similar to Machiaveli's idea of *virtû*.[16] It also approaches Vico's "common nature of nations," which is "a psychological unity" or a mutual state of members of a society: a unity that is reflected in governments, religions, laws, and customs.[17]

The following dimensions of Ibn Khaldun's concept of *asabiyah* are now presented in some detail:

1. *Asabiyah* is not confined to nomadism as some writers believe,[18] although it is stronger among nomads than among sedentary people. Ibn Khaldun used it as a core of historical explanation of social life in the nomadic and urban societies. It will be seen that his theory is centered mainly around the concept of *asabiyah* and its role in the transition from one of these two societies to the other. (See Chapters 5–8.)

2. *Asabiyah* is not necessarily based on blood relation. Man is naturally inclined to help his relatives. Whether the rela-

tion is true or false in reality does not matter in this regard; what actually matters is the social consideration. At this point, Ibn Khaldun regained his usual sociological insight.[19]

He recognized the social solidarity in groups other than the family and the tribe, especially since *asabiyah* comes about through social interaction, "through long reciprocal testing and trying, and through the activities of common occupations."[20]

3. *Asabiyah* is natural and universal. It is not confined to Arab people. Ibn Khaldun identified the *asabiyahs* of several non-Arab peoples such as Persians, Jews, Assyrians, Greeks, Romans, Turks, and Berbers.[21]

4. *Asabiyah* is related to the economic structure of society. Rabi' considerd it one of the several phenomena whose characteristics and development are effects of the prevailing mode of living in a society. He sees a dialectical interplay between economic and cultural elements of social solidarity: No abstract polarization of cause and effect can be found in Ibn Khaldun's study of *asabiyah* in *badawa* (nomadism-ruralism) and *hadara* (urbanism). "While primitive and vigorous *asabiyah*, with all its pecularities, is an effect of the way of living under *badawa*,[22] it acts in due time as the principal cause of changing this very way of living to a completely different one under *hadara*."[23]

5. A strong relationship exists between *asabiyah* and religion as a social institution and as a means of social control. Religion strengthens group solidarity, an idea emphasized by Durkheim some 500 years later. Durkheim believed that religion provides a social solidarity, a cohesion, a "oneness"; it unites members of society together, hence maintaining the society itself.[24] However, Vico's statement that "if religion is lost among the people, they have nothing left to enable them to live in society,"[25] is in sharp contrast to Ibn Khaldun's conviction that human society can exist and persist without religion.

Ibn Khaldun's emphasis on the social function of religion to unify people can be seen in the achievement of the Arabs after they became Muslims. When the Arab tribal spirit (*asabiyah*) coincided with certain aspects of religion, the Arabs became extremely religious. They, Ibn Khaldun rationalized, showed amazing zeal,[26] sincerity, and devotion to Islam when after

Muhammad's death their *asabiyah* was directed against the "unbelievers" outside Arabia.

Ibn Khaldun realized that religion itself requires *asabiyah* or social solidarity. Religious movements without *asabiyah* are ineffective. He provided us with several cases showing the significance of *asabiyah* in the success of religious reforms.[27]

6. *Asabiyah* exercises a profound influence upon polity. A dynasty or state cannot be established except with a strong *asabiyah*. When this *asabiyah* is lost and when all powerful members of the state are wiped out, a great disintegration sets in.[28] Hence, the aspirations of the state's members are proportionate to the strength of their government and its superiority over the people. These aspirations remain with them until the final destruction of the state.[29] The aspects of *asabiyah* in relation to polity may be summarized as follows:

a. Leadership exists only through superiority, and superiority only through *asabiyah*.

b. The individual needs his group's (government's) cooperation and protection, because he shares the same *asabiyah* of the group.

c. Weapons may strengthen a group, but something else is also needed for defense against aggression, a strong sense of solidarity and loyalty to the group, *i.e., asabiyah*.

d. *Asabiyah* does not preclude aggressiveness. Injustice and aggression are parts of human nature.

e. *Asabiyah* is much more than just a social power. Strong *asabiyah* also indicates good character and high qualifications of relationship, such as the forgiveness of error, tolerance toward the weak, attentiveness to the complaints of supplicants, fulfillment of the duties of the religious law and divine worship in all details, and avoidance of fraud, cunning, and deceit. A basic qualification of a good ruler is that he will be well informed about, and well acquainted with, the holders of *asabiyah* and willing to respect their positions;[30] hence, the mutual respect between, and reciprocal adjustment of, leaders and followers. (See Chapter 5.)

f. *Asabiyah*, and for this matter the life span of a state, depend on numerical strength.[31]

g. The state or urban government is the goal of *asabiyah*.

This particular aspect deserves further explication.

For Ibn Khaldun, a state's foundation is the goal of *asabiyah*, and urbanism is the goal of the nomadic people. Because these people possess a strong *asabiyah*, they can achieve this goal. Once they achieve life's bare necessities, they begin to seek comforts, luxuries, and softness of sedentary life. Thus, establishing a state without urbanization is inconceivable; and the existence of urbanism without sedentary culture is also impossible. Sedentary culture (*e.g.* refined knowledge of the crafts), cannot exist without luxury. Luxury is the result of wealth; wealth is a consequence of the establishment of a state, an interwoven cyclical relationship. Ibn Khaldun generalized that the larger a state, the more important is its sedentary culture.[32]

Such a settlement of people (in urban settings) makes them a target of political domination. Because of the ruler's superiority, their submissiveness and obedience are expected. They may not even be able to leave their districts and go to other regions, because such regions are already inhabited by other people who took them away from someone and kept others out.[33]

Ibn Khaldun appeared to have considered *asabiyah* the driving force in human society's development. *Asabiyah* may be a significant, fundamental, and crucial phenomenon; however, it is not the only criterion for society's development.

Furthermore, *asabiyah* seems to be the core of the Khaldunian social theory,[34] but, as will be mentioned later, this theory cannot be fully explained without taking into consideration the conflict between *badawa* and *hadara* which is one major consequence of the *asabiyah* itself.

Some students of Ibn Khaldun's thought consider his theory of *asabiyah* a worship of power for its own sake. This is not so. When he required a strong *asabiyah* for a leader, he did not mean simply that might makes right. *Asabiyah* is mostly a nomadic trait, and Ibn Khaldun studied it in its nomadic context. The nomadic *shaykh* who has a strong *asabiyah* is usually a good leader.[35] In his person might *and* right normally go hand in hand. *Asabiyah* then, as has been shown, is much more than just a social power; strong *asabiyah* also indicates good character and high qualifications of leadership.

Ibn Khaldun lived in a society dominated by nomadic values. He also lived among the desert Bedouins and observed how *asabiyah* is most strongly marked among them. His *Muqaddimah* provides ample examples of how *asabiyah* influences social relations. Two of these examples are presented here:

1. In spite of his relatively strong rationalistic tendency, Muhammad was unable to influence the minds of the nomadic Arabs. After thirteen years of vehement preaching and arguing, only one nomad (Abu Dhar)[36] was converted to his religion. Yet, afterwards, when Islam brought victory to its converts, the Arabian nomads entered it, as *the Koran* puts it, "in shoals."[37] Almost all the tribes of Arabia sent their delegations to Muhammad declaring their adoption of Islam.[38]

2. Ibn Khaldun flatly denounced those religious troublemakers who, under the influence of some idealistic thinking, often disturb society. They will eventually perish because of their ignorance of the rule of *asabiyah*.[39] When he discussed the Muhammadan doctrine of "bidding the good and forbidding the evil," on which these troublemakers often base their campaigns, Ibn Khaldun considered it a duty that concerns only those who are *able* to do it. If one is unable to bid the good or forbid the evil openly, he should do so within his heart. *Ability* here is defined largely in terms of *asabiyah*. Ibn Khaldun repeatedly and emphatically advocated that Allah never orders man to do anything that is unable to do.[40] If man has no *asabiyah* or a strong party to support him in his bidding the good or forbidding the evil, he then should submit to whatever the holders of *asabiyah* dictate, good or evil. In fact, this is what Ibn Khaldun did.

Note, however, that although Ibn Khaldun acknowledged that *asabiyah* cannot exist without a group, he admitted that a group may exist without *asabiyah*. Submissiveness and docility can break the strength of *asabiyah*; people tend to be submissive only when they are unable to defend themselves or unable to attack.[41] Ibn Khaldun provided the example of the Israelites whom Moses summoned and told to conquer Syria. Because they were too weak, they said: "Behold therein is a people of giants, and behold we shall not set foot into it until they have left it, *i.e.*, until God drives them away from there, by defeating them through his power . . . . When Moses implored them, they became rebellious, and said, 'Go thou and thy Lord, and fight.'"[42] The Israelites needed boldness and intrepidy, which Ibn Khaldun regarded as essential ingredients for this type of asabiyah.

Moreover, Ibn Khaldun admitted that establishing a dynasty in lands that are "free" from asabiyah is possible. "Government there will be a tranquil affair, because seditions and rebellions are few, and the dynasty there does not need much [asabiyah]."[43] This was the case in Egypt and Spain in Ibn Khaldun's time. Polity in Egypt was most powerful and firmly rooted because Egypt had few dissidents.[44]

Had Ibn Khaldun lived many years longer, he would have noticed that the Ottomans (Turks), for instance, emerged from central Asia with an esprit de corps other than a tribal one.[45] The same was also true of other Western groups that dominated his own homeland. In addition, a modern army equipped with modern weapons is usually able to crush any nomadic uprising based on asabiyah, which is what happened to a powerful nomadic group in Najd (Saudi Arabia) in the late eighteenth century. Although, at the beginning of the twentieth century, this very same group tried again and this time was successful in establishing a state, which was maintained largely by the discovery of oil in its desert, this example can be considered an exception.

Nevertheless, had Ibn Khaldun witnessed the great wealth accumulated by some Arab states, he would have assured us of his theory's validity, that wealth without asabiyah makes the Arabs incapable of defending themselves against their enemies or even pressing their claims, however right they might be. For him, right without might is inconceivable. Moreover, evidence of the influence of asabiyah and nomadic values on the political life in the Arab world is stil obvious. Gellner observed that as late as the 1950s the Moroccan tribes joined political parties, and swore an oath of loyalty to them, as tribal units, and that in Yemen "the political significance of tribes increased in the twentieth century rather than declined."[46] In Kuwait, the 1985 parliamentary election indicated that thousands of people were clearly following tribal lore. And alluding to the dogfight, in late June 1984, in which Saudi jetfighters shot down an Iranian warplane, Saudi Arabian Prince Sultan declared that the world "respects nothing but the right that is supported by might."[47] Ibn Khaldun saw no conflict between might and right: The institution of *asabiyah* successfully combines the two.

Chapter 5

THE RISE AND DECLINE
OF THE STATE

This chapter discusses the state, the most significant consequence of a strong *asabiyah* (social solidarity.) The requirements
of good rulership, the shortcomings of the ruler, and the factors
contributing to the state's disintegration are presented in some
detail. Ibn Khaldun's major political thoughts are briefly compared with those of several Western thinkers.

The state "is the natural goal" of *asabiyah*. As mentioned
before, the importance and strength of *asabiyah*, in Ibn
Khaldun's opinion, may result from close and direct blood relationships. However, the state is more than just blood relationships and more than just leadership; it "means superiority and
the power to rule by force."[1]

Ibn Khaldun emphasized the idea that once *asabiyah* has
established superiority over the people who share it, it will, by
its very nature, seek superiority over people of other *asabiyahs*
unrelated to the first. If an *asabiyah* overpowers another
asabiyah and makes it subservient to itself, the defeated one
gives added power to the victorious one, which, as a result, sets
its goal of domination higher than before. It comes to share the
prosperity and abundance with those who have been in possession of these things for a long time.[2] The weak people will have
to submit to this new power, for such people are also "concerned

with prosperity, gain, and a life of abundance. They are satisfied to lead an easy, restful life in the shadow of the ruling dynasty."[3] However, if an *asabiyah* is equal to another in strength, each will have to maintain its sway over its own domain and people, as is the case with tribes and nations all over the world.[4]

Because of its social implications, the state is, according to Ibn Khaldun, a natural social institution that cannot survive except through social organization and cooperation. "Therefore, it is necessary to have reference to ordained political norms, which are accepted by the mass and to whose laws it submits."[5] Moreover, as an institution, "government becomes a reality when there is a ruler who rules over subjects and handles their affairs."[6]

Ibn Khaldun discussed the purpose of the caliphate and the conditions governing it, but he did not specify that the caliphate is the best possible form of state. The caliphate preserves religion and the exercise of the state's political leadership. Four conditions govern the institution of the *imamate* (religious leadership): knowledge, probity, competence, and freedom of the senses from any defect that might affect judgement and action. Ibn Khaldun explained in some detail each of these conditions. For example, the *imam's* (religious leader's) knowledge "is satisfactory only if he is able to make independent decisions," because "blind acceptance of tradition is a shortcoming."[7]

Ibn Khaldun emphasized the point that the restraining influence is a function of any type of government, *i.e.*, it could be maintained "even if there is no religious law."[8] This idea comes close to the position taken by the Mu'tazilah who thought that when Muslims agree upon the practice of justice and observance of divine laws no *imam* is needed, and the position of *imam* is no longer necessary. The importance of religion in political leadership cannot be denied, however. Ibn Khaldun stated that Arabs can obtain political power only by making use of some "religious coloring." They are unable to establish a state or successfully manage it without a religion. Their pride and roughness normally makes their unification into a large state difficult; but when, under the influence of religion, they are "fully united as a social organization," they can achieve miracles. Their roughness is then directed toward outsiders. Based on religion, the government at the beginning of its establishment tends to be kind in the exercise of power and just in its administration. Later, it will endeavor to coerce the subjects and thus it becomes a "bad government."[9]

Qualities of Rulership

People must have a ruler who will cause them "to act in accordance with what is good for them and who will prevent them by force from doing things harmful to them."[10] They are not interested in the ruler's personal traits such as "his good figure, handsome face, large frame, wide knowledge, good handwriting, or acute mind;" rather, they are interested in his relation to them. A basic qualification of a good ruler is that he be well informed about, and well acquainted with, the members of his group.[11] Mutual respect between, and reciprocal adjustment of, leaders and followers constitute an important aspect of *asabiyah*. The leader's qualities may include humility in dealing with his people and "respect for their feelings." Once he considers them despicable, they usually revolt against him and despise him.[12] Ibn Khaldun, like Pigors, classified rulers into leaders and dominators. Where domination prevails, no place for *asabiyah* exists. Ibn Khaldun clearly showed that as soon as domination begins to replace leadership in a dynasty, the *asabiyah* gradually loses its vigor and its binding force and eventually dies out. Consequently, the ruler should not be misled by the idealistic formula "to each man according to what he absolutely deserves"; the ruler rather, should follow the dictum of expediency, that is, "to each man according to his relative power."

Mildness in political behavior is also a significant trait of good rulership. If the ruler is mild and overlooks the shortcomings of his subjects, they will trust and like him. If he uses force and always thinks of punishment as a means of exposing the faults of his people, then his subjects become depressed and fearful and seek to protect themselves against him through lies, ruses, and deceit.[13] Ibn Khaldun, however, was quick to realize that "mildness is usually found in careless and unconcerned persons."[14]

As for the ruler's intelligence, Ibn Khaldun contended that "it is a drawback in a political leader to be too clever and shrewd." Instead, the middle road is praiseworthy.[15] Ibn Khaldun did not prefer a very intelligent ruler because such a ruler tends to overlook the needs of his subjects and neglect their feelings. He "imposes tasks upon his subjects that are beyond their ability, because he is aware of things they do not perceive and, through his genius, foresees the outcome of things at the start." People should not, therefore, be victims of his intelligence, because this quality is "accompanied by tyrannical and bad rulership" and by a tendency to make the people do things that are against their nature. Accordingly, to see a ruler deviate from what is right is not surprising. This, again, shows the necessity for established political norms that the populace must abide by to keep the state alive and to make their society a going concern.[16]

The ruler alone may not be able to handle the office of the state. He must look for help from his fellow men. The help may come from people close to him, e.g., through common descent. Otherwise, "principal governmental ranks and functions" may be distributed to qualified persons.[17] Ibn Khaldun felt that "scholars are, of all people, those least familiar with the ways of politics." They "are used to mental speculation and to a searching study of ideas which they abstract from the sensibilia and conceive in their minds as general universals," which may not conform to reality.[18] Conversely, politicians must pay attention to the facts of the outside world and the conditions attaching to and depending on politics."[19] Although this statement cannot be accepted in its entirety, one must understand Ibn Khaldun's emphasis on "the average person of a healthy disposition and a mediocre intelligence," who restricts himself to daily matters as they are and judges every situation "by its particular circumstances." That is, the ruler's judgment "is not infected with analogy and generalization. Most of his speculation stops at matters perceivable by the senses, and he does not go beyond them in his mind."[20] Therefore, such a ruler can be trusted when he reflects upon his political activities.

Briefly, an important and necessary condition for the individual in charge of the affairs of the state is that he belongs to people who possess a strong *asabiyah* that helps him force his subjects to follow the rulership of the state and, if possible, to unite them for effective protection. A strong *umma* (nation) is capable of expansion. "Such a nation is better able to achieve superiority and full control, and to subdue other groups. The members of such a nation have the strength to fight other nations."[21] It would, however, be difficult for a state to establish itself firmly in an area where there are different groups, *e.g.*, tribes, that oppose the state or rebel against it.[22]

When the state is firmly established, it can dispense with *asabiyah*. As a result, injustice prevails. An example of injustice detrimental to the state's existence is the exercise of political power through commerce, agriculture, or the crafts. A ruler's commercial activity is an unnatural means of livelihood and harmful to his subjects. Ibn Khaldun described this type of activity in some detail:

> This is a great error. It causes harm to the subjects in many ways. First, farmers and merchants will find it difficult to buy livestock and merchandise and to procure cheaply the things that belong to farming and commerce. The subjects have all the same or approximately the same amount of wealth. Competition between them already exhausts, or comes close to exhausting, their financial resources. Now, when the ruler, who has so much more money than they, competes with them, scarcely a single one of them will any longer be able to obtain the things he wants, and everybody will become worried and unhappy.
>
> Furthermore, the ruler can appropriate much of the agricultural products and the available merchandise, if it occurs to him. He can do it by force, or by buying things up at the cheapest possible price . . . . There may be no one who would dare to bid against him. Thus, he will be able to force the seller to lower his price. Further, when agricultural products . . . or goods of any kind, become available, the ruler cannot wait for a favorable market and a boom, because he has to take care of government needs. Therefore, he forces the merchants or farmers who deal in these particular products to buy from him. He will be satisfied only with the highest prices . . . . The mer-

chants and farmers, on the other hand, will exhaust their liquid capital in such transactions. The merchandise they thus acquire will remain useless on their hands. They themselves will no longer be able to trade, which is what enables them to earn something and make their living. Often, they need money. Then, they have to sell the goods that they were forced to buy from the ruler, at the lowest prices, during a slump in the market. Often, the merchant or farmer has to do the same thing over again. He thus exhausts his capital and has to go out of business.[23]

Ibn Khaldun clearly observed that the ruler is often influenced to choose such a course by the merchants and farmers themselves.[24]

Another unnatural means of livelihood, according to Ibn Khaldun, is the ruler's extortion of the state's money that comes mainly from revenues. This concept will be discussed later in this chapter.

A third unnatural activity occurs when government high officials "try to escape from government control and go to some other region with the government property they have acquired." There, they have "the opportunity to spend and enjoy their money in greater safety."[25] This means of livelihood is unnatural because, Ibn Khaldun emphasized, their money is not a profit that is the value normally realized from their labor.[26]

A fourth unnatural activity, regarded by Ibn Khaldun as "one of the greatest injustices and one which contributes most to the destruction of civilization, is the unjustified imposition of tasks and the use of the subjects for forced labor. This is because labor belongs to the things that constitute capital."[27]

The fifth unnatural and unjustified activity is "the confiscation of money or other property from the owners, without compensation and without cause."[28] Ibn Khaldun believed that "the religious law legalizes the use of cunning in trading, but forbids depriving people of their property illegally."[29] Any activity by the government that is dictated by force or the free play of the power of wrathfulness is injustice, tyranny, and reprehensible by both the religious law and the requirements of political wisdom. A political power, e.g., a government, normally causes people to act as required by rational insight into the means of furthering their worldly interests, whereas the religious rule, *e.g.*, the caliphate, causes "the masses to act as required by religious insight into their interests in the other world as well as in this world."[30] Once religion ceases to be effective, tyranny and injustice are expected. In Islam, the millenial hope or Mahdism has been the refuge from injustice. Modern students of Islam believe that the idea of the Mahdi was developed in Islam during the Umayyad period under the influence of Jewish and Christian Messianism.[31] Both Messiah and Mahdi have almost the same meaning. *Messiah* means the anointed one, and *Mahdi* means "the divinely guided one,"[32] who, like the Messiah, will appear in the future to deliver people from the prevailing social injustice.

Factors for the Decline of the State

According to Ibn Khaldun, the state must be built upon two foundations: (1) *asabiyah*, which finds its expression in force and soldiers; and (2) money, which supports force and maintains government functions. "Disintegration befalls the state at these two foundations." The first foundation is especially emphasized throughout *The Muqaddimah*. *Asabiyah* may differ from one group to another; but even the strongest *asabiyah* can be weakened by luxury. Luxury also can wear out the state and overthrow it.[33] In more detail, Ibn Khaldun views the main factors for the decline of the state as follows:

1. *The weakening of the religious influence*:　Religion usually makes people unite, agree on issues, and even press their claims. This is especially true at the beginning of the state's establishment when religion provides another power in addition to that of *asabiyah*. At that stage, nothing can withstand these people because their outlook is one, and they are ready to die for their common objectives. Once this religious coloring changes, the group or the state is annihilated. The Arabs "have neglected the religion. Thus, they became ineffective in political leadership."[34] They are the least willing of all people to subordinate themselves to each other, as they are proud, ambitious,

and eager to be the leaders. Through religion they have some restraining influence in themselves. Religion encourages them to unite as a social organization and makes them obtain superiority and political power.

The weakening of the religious influence not only leads to the decline of political power, but also can lead to "tyranny and injustice."[35]

2. *Luxury*:   At first, luxury is prolific and produces benefits which in turn provide additional strength to a state, including an increased number of clients and followers. However, "those who are singled out to support the dynasty indulge in a life of ease and sink into luxury and plenty. They make servants of their fellows and contemporaries and use them to further the various interests and enterprises of the dynasty."[36] Servants are needed by most of those wo were brought up accustomed to luxury and are too proud to take care of their needs or are unable to do so. Although Ibn Khaldun was against using people for this "lower level" of occupation, he also believed that "satisfactory and trustworthy servants are almost nonexistent."[37]

With more luxuries, the toughness of the citizen's life is lost, *asabiyah* and courage weaken, and the offspring will have disdain for all things necessary to maintain *asabiyah*. *Asabiyah* and courage decrease even further in the next generations. Eventually, *asabiyah* is altogether destroyed. "The greater their luxury and the easier the life they enjoy, the closer they are to extinction"[38] as an original group.

3. *The ruler's reliance on helpers and partisans from groups unrelated to the state or to his asabiyah*:   Those helpers are known for their toughness, and accordingly he uses them as an army, believing that they will be better able to suffer the hardships of wars, hunger, and privation. In actuality, "the ruler seeks the help of clients and followers against the men of his own people."[39] As a result of luxury, leisure, and the mutual hatred between the ruler and his own people, who are proud of the noteworthy achievements of their forefathers, the ruler becomes independent of his people. In order to prevent them from seizing power, the ruler cares only for his new followers. He singles out the helpers for preference and many honors, distributes among them property, and confers upon them the

most important administrative positions. This situation, Ibn Khaldun believed, announces the destruction of the state. (See Chapter 6.)

4. *Seclusion of, and control over, the ruler by others:* Because of the ruler's dependence upon people not related to him by common *asabiyah*, and because of his indulgence in luxury, it is possible that his close associates and entourage gain power, and take over the throne or the political organization. It is also possible that the ruler may be secluded and deprived of all political power. He may contrive to escape from his situation. If he is successful in this endeavor then his revenge is expected, either by killing his opponent "or by merely deposing him." Ibn Khaldun observed that the latter case happens very rarely.[40]

5. *Tyranny:* When the ruler's power is firmly established, he begins to claim all the glory for himself alone. He also endeavors to remain aloof from the common people as much as possible; for this reason, he appoints a person whose sole function is to prevent people from having access to him (the ruler). The ruler confines his association to his friends. During his rulership, he may develop peculiar qualities that may not be known even to persons in contact with him. These persons are usually punished if they do something that the ruler does not like. He also starts to humiliate and kill those who helped him attain power through *asabiyah*, because his envy of them changes to fear.[41] "That is what happened to every nation (*umma*) that fell under the yoke of tyranny and learned through it the meaning of injustic."[42] Because of tyranny, the ruler normally develops egotism (*ta'alluh*) which he endeavors to maintain.[43]

It should be understood, Ibn Khaldun emphasized, that "politics requires that only one person exercise control." When various individuals exercise it, disintegration and destruction of the state could result as a consequence of possible differences among each other.[44] It seems that this conclusion is based upon his observation and investigation of the nature and scope of the political process in more than one state, where the leader alone takes charge until he leaves no part in the power to anyone else." This, according to Ibn Khaldun, is an inevitable political phenomenon.[45]

Ibn Khaldun observed that "it is difficult and impossible to escape from official life after having once been in it."[46] To illustrate his views, he provided examples about the Arabs. "Every Arab is eager to be the leader. Scarcely a one of them would cede his power to another, even to his father, his brother, or the eldest most important member of his family. That happens only in rare cases and under pressure of considerations of decency."[47]

6. *The encroachment of political instability into economic conditions:* The relationship between polity and economy is clearly shown in *The Muqaddimah*. This is especially true in the interrelationship between the decline of the state and the deterioration of economic life.

Ibn Khaldun stated that at the early period of the statehood, the revenues are distributed among the subjects who share in the ruler's *asabiyah*. The ruler's share "is restricted to the very small amount he needs." Once he obtains control over his subjects, he prevents them from getting the revenues which have been allocated to them. Instead he supports his clients and followers who support and defend his rule and his power. As a result of their support, the need for more revenues becomes an urgent matter. The inner circle and entourage, however, spend the money for a purpose for which it was not intended. Consequently, the ruler becomes of the opinion that he is more entitled than they to the wealth. He takes the money and appropriates it for himself. At this stage, the state becomes detestable to his inner circle and, in turn, the state suffers therefrom. "It loses its entourage and great personalities and its rich and wealthy intimates. A great part of the edifice of glory crumbles, after having been supported and built up to a great height by those who shared in it."[48]

Ibn Khaldun stressed the point that as a consequence of the luxury, expenditures, and the insufficiency of the revenue to pay for its needs, the state may find itself in financial straits.[49] It may find itself imposing customs duties, or increasing the kinds of customs duties, on the commercial activities of its people. "Sometimes, it applies torture to its officials and tax collectors and sucks their bones dry of a part of their fortune. This happens when officials and tax collectors are observed to have appropriated a good deal of tax money, which their accounts do not show."[50]

For Ibn Khaldun, the state's decline is equivalent to senility, which "cannot be cured or made to disappear because it is something natural, and natural things do not change."[51] As a result, the power is taken over by a group that has a strong *asabiyah*. Possibly, the leadership "'goes to some person from the lowest class of people. He obtains [*asabiyah*] and close contact with the mob."[52]

Ibn Khaldun observed that the state is stronger at its center. "When it has reached its farthest expansion, it becomes too weak and incapable to go any farther . . . . When the dynasty becomes senile and weak, it begins to crumble at its extremities."[53] Provincial governors in the state, before others, endeavor to gain control over remote or outlying regions.[54]

When people lose their *asabiyah*, they become meek, docile, and too weak to defend themselves; "they become the victims of anyone who tries to dominate them, and a prey to anyone who has the appetite."[55] Briefly, they suffer humiliation and indigence.[56]

Ibn Khaldun and Other Social Thinkers

Several writers before Ibn Khaldun dealt with the government as a political institution. The conflict between the "temple" and the "palace" which H. G. Wells described in his discussion of the Summerian civilization[57] can be found in one form or another whenever a civilization or a secular society arises. In spite of the fact that Ibn Khaldun observed only an autocratic rule, his analysis of the state is considered superior to that of Plato and Aristotle. Unlike the Greek philosophers, he did not discuss the best, or the ideal, form of government, and he separated politics from ethics. And unlike Muslim thinkers his thought-style is more secular than sacred. This is evidenced in their interpretations of the political systems. In *al-Medina al-Fadilah*, al-Farabi depicted an ideal state, and so did Ikhwan al-

Safa (Brethren of Purity) in their *Rasa'il*.[58] For Ibn Khaldun, "the 'ideal city' of the philosophers is something rare and remote. They discuss it as a hypothesis.[59]

Ibn Khaldun's political thought can be compared with that of some Western thinkers.

First, one can compare Ibn Khaldun and Machiavelli as able statesmen whose experienced isolation from public service inspired the former to compose his *Muqaddimah* and helped the latter to write *The Prince*. Both thinkers had witnessed the decline of their states, the first in North Africa and the second in Italy. Thus, both failed to see a strong, well-etablished state. Specifically: (1.) Both thinkers described and analyzed the main qualities of the rulers, the good ones and the bad ones. For Machiavelli, the ideal prince or statesman is a tyrant who resorts to the most ruthless means in maintaining his power. Hence the gloomy stamp which brands Machiavellian policy even today.[60] However, Machiavelli admitted that "principalities are in danger when the prince from the position of a civil rule changes to an absolute one . . . therefore a wise prince will seek means by which his subjects will always be faithful to him."[61] (2.) Both went beyond philosophical ideas of Plato and Aristotle by maintaining a complete separation of ethics from politics. Moreover, by separating the state from religious influ-ence, Ibn Khaldun's and Machiavelli's attitudes toward the state can be characterized as secular. (3.) Both observed the danger of relying upon mercenaries, who are seen as useless. In the long run, mercenaries cause the dismantling of the state, because they are "without discipline, faithless, bold amongst friends, cowardly amongst enemies."[62] (4.) Ibn Khaldun's con-cept of *asabiyah* approaches Machiavelli's idea of *virtù*. Specifically, both thinkers stressed political solidarity as the in-dispensable source of power for success in politics and war.[63] For both, power is, generally a natural phenomenon, a natural force. However, when one read *the Prince* and *The Muqaddimah*, a major difference can be seen in that Ibn Khaldun stressed the social dimension more than did Machiavelli. One can detect a sociological touch in Ibn Khaldun's writing, and his generaliza-tions on political life are more comprehensive and more realistic than are those of Machiavelli.

Ibn Khaldun also can be compared with Jean Bodin (1530-1596). Both agreed that the state is developed out of force; an idea emphasized by later social scientists, *e.g.*, Lester Ward, Sumner, Gumplowicz, and Oppenheimer, who believed that the state is based upon oppression, exploitation, and social inequality.[64] And for both thinkers, processes of social disorganization and reorganization are facts of human society. Other similarities of thought between the two thinkers can be seen in their works on historical interpretation of society and culture. The resemblance some of Bodin's doctrines bear to those of Ibn Khaldun might have been as a result of culture contact, but this assumption warrants further investigation.[65] Even if a connection is found between the thoughts of Ibn Khaldun and Bodin, minimizing the latter's contribution to social thought, especially in areas other than the state, is unfair.

A brief comparison of Ibn Khaldun and Vico indicates that both saw the government as natural and necessary. They agreed that an end to government is always found, including the savage or dictatorial form. The next chapter presents a detailed discussion of the similarities between Vico's and Ibn Khaldun's ideas concering the rise and fall of civilization.

Montesquieu also, like Ibn Khaldun, stressed the idea that people need a powerful group to protect them, that a despotic ruler "only thinks of promoting his own interest."[66] They despised slavery, but Montesquieu was more explicit in disliking domination and tyranny. He went into great detail in viewing the despotic government as lacking "fundamental laws" that require "the most passive obedience,"[67] and as being subject to a continual corruption."[68] Here again Montesquieu was more explicit than Ibn Khaldun in showing how under such a rule the very best laws became bad.[69] Both thinkers contended that "mild" (as Ibn Khaldun put it) or "sound" (as Montesquieu stated) rule has a positive effect on people.[70] Like Ibn Khaldun, Montesquieu discussed the question of the involvement of the government and leaders in business; they emphatically declared that the prince or leader should refrain from such activity.

Some of Comte's ideas also converge with those of Ibn Khaldun: (1) Both thinkers treated the subject of the state from the historical and analytical viewpoints. (2) Both clearly stated that social division of labor is inevitable for the state's development and growth. This point has been greatly emphasized by Durkheim. Ibn Khaldun, Durkheim, and Simmel all agreed that the government usually selects the best-suited individuals for positions of authority.[71] (3) It must be emphasized here that Ibn Khaldun and Comte witnessed the disintegration of the old social order, and both were hoping for a stable state that could maintain a needed social control. This can be seen in Ibn Khaldun's emphasis on the role of *asabiyah* in strengthening the social group, and in Comte's analysis of society as an organism where the whole is better known and more important than the parts.[72]

Like Ibn Khaldun, Oppenheimer emphasized the significance of satisfying economic needs in the struggle to achieve political goals.[73] Oppenheimer's rationale for the state's development is as follows: Herdmen gradually become accustomed to earning their livelihood through warfare, and this "warlike character of the nomad is a great factor in the creation of states. Herdmen become parts of a state structure only when they find in their neighborhoods an evolved economic organization which they can subjugate."[74] It seems here as if one is reading pages from *The Muqaddimah.*

According to Weber, although a nation is apt to include notions of common descent and homogeneity, *e.g.,* common-cultural values that provide a unifying national bond, "national affiliation need not be based upon common blood."[75] This statement seems to echo Ibn Khaldun's ideas previously expressed in this chapter, especially his notion that the state is more than just a blood relationship. Both men dealt with traditional authority and provided ample examples to illustrate their views. They agreed that the person in power is not a *dominator* but a *ruler* or simply a mere *chief.*[76] Ibn Khaldun clearly stated that this is especially true in nomadic life.

Ibn Khaldun's attitude toward the state was secular. The state is a natural phenomenon whose main functions are social control and social benevolence. His political observations are, to a large extent, pertinent to current political life. Witnessing today's political events in several countries of the Middle East, North Africa, and the Third World, demonstrates how vivid Ibn

Khaldun's analysis of the political situation is, especially his characterization of the autocratic rule and the resultant injustice which he considered detrimental to the state's existence.

Chapter 6

THE CYCLICAL PATTERN: HISTORY AS A CYCLE

This chapter deals with the phases of a state's decline, the last of which leads to the formation or rise of a new state. The Khaldunian cyclical theory is compared with other theories developed by Vico, Turgot, Marx, Gumplowicz, Spengler, Sorokin, and Toynbee who also investigated the subject of history as a cycle.

According to Ibn Khaldun, the state's decline leads to anarchy which, in turn, destroys civilization. This process is a result of the transition from the primitive life of *badawa* (nomadism-ruralism) to the civilized life of *hadara* (urbanism). This change begins as the nomads are lured and attracted by the city's luxuries. Their leader tends to gather more and more *asabiyahs* before attacking some of the neighboring states and establishing a new one. This process appears inescapable as long as some contact exists between nomadic tribes and city dwellers.

For Ibn Khaldun, the state undergoes five stages or phases. The first is that of overcoming the enemy and the adversary and taking possession of command "by tearing it away from the hands of the former state." In this stage, the ruler serves as a model to his followers by the manner in which he collects taxes, defends and protects the territory, and by not isolating himself from them in any way. The second stage is one in which the ruler governs his people autocratically and isolates himself from them. He endeavors to gain numerous vassals and followers in order to humiliate the bearers of his *asabiyah* and his kin, who claim an equal share with him in governing the state. By keeping them away from power, he is able to keep it and its glory in his own family. He is now supported by a small number of individuals who are "strangers," not related to him by blood or tribal affiliation. The third stage is one of leisure and tranquil life. It is also one in which human beings aspire to acquire wealth and to perpetuate themselves through monuments. The ruler utilizes all his strength to collect taxes, to regulate revenues and expenditures, and to calculate the costs of constructing huge buildings, large monuments, and spacious cities. At the same time, he is generous to his followers and his attendants with money and honors depending on their positions. He inspects his troops and provides them with ample material assistance in addition to their monthly allowances. The effect can be seen in their dress, their ornaments, and their arms on festive days. Thus, he can impress allied states and frighten hostile ones. This stage is the last in which the ruler governs autocratically and makes his decision independently. The fourth stage is one of contentment and peacefulness. The ruler is satisfied with what his predecessors have accomplished. He lives in peace with his royal peers and enemies. He imitates his predecessors by exactly following in their footsteps, believing that if he does not do so his authority would be destroyed. The fifth stage is one of wastefulness and lavishness. In this stage, the ruler destroys what his predecessors have built as a result of his lusts, pleasures, and generosity to his inner circle. He surrounds himself with "false friends and evil individuals" to whom he entrusts enormous tasks of the state they are not qualified to handle; "they do not know what to do and what not to do." He mistreats the nobles and well-known clients of his people as well as his predecessors' followers. These people become angry with him and no longer support him. Moreover, he loses some of his troops by spending their allowances for his pleasures and by remaining aloof. This is the way he destroys what his predecessors had found and demolishes what they had established. Consequently, decline sets in in the state, and chronic disease takes hold of it, for which there is almost no cure; thus, the state perishes.[1]

The decline of a state means the rise of a new one. The clash between *badawa*, and *hadara* results in a cyclical rise and fall of states that is also dialectical in that each new stage arises from the conflicting contradictions of the previous one. The change in states is due to a complex dialectical interplay between the economic base of society and such factors as *asabiyah*. No strict causal determinism can be found in Ibn Khaldun's study of *asabiyah* in the *badawa* and *hadara*. In the transition from *badawa* to *hadara*, causes become effects and effects become causes.[2] Suffice it to say, that for Ibn Khaldun two basic conditions underly the dialectical basis of change:

1. Some type of polarization should be found in the value systems of the two cultures between which dialectical interaction takes place. Each culture should possess certain characteristics that the other normally lacks. Thus, a cyclical movement may arise as a result of the desire of each culture to seek in the other what it lacks in itself.

2. Within each culture, a polarization should exist between what it possesses and what it lacks.[3]

To Ibn Khaldun, a state's life cycle has the same inescapable stages as an individual's. It has its birth, youth, old age, and death. An average state normally contains four successive kings. Simon is correct in stating that Ibn Khaldun's four-generation pattern is not ascribed or fixed; rather, it is a model.[4] "The rule of four generations with respect to prestige usually holds true. It may happen that a 'house' is wiped out, disappears, and collapses in fewer than four generations, or it may continue unto the fifth or sixth generations, though in a state of decline and decay."[5] In fact, in another section of *The Muqaddimah*, Ibn Khaldun admitted that this had not been the case with some nations like the Persians, "who had a period of thousands of years." The same was also true of the Copts, Nabataens, the Romans, and the first Arabs;[6] hence *asabiyah's* influence in forming, and maintaining, the state. If *asabiyah* is strong, the state is also strong. When *asabiyah* is weak, it is a sign that the state would cease to exist and its power will be taken by people whose *asabiyah* is strong.

The prime mover behind the Khaldunian social dialectic is then the *asabiyah* – not the individual efforts he regarded as useless. *Asabiyah* came to play the same role as did Allah's will to the Sufites.[7] This does not mean that Ibn Khaldun denied the effect of Allah's will upon social process. In fact, he, as a devout Muslim, firmly believed that Allah's will is behind every natural and social phenomenon; however, Allah does not usually do things in contradiction to the laws He has created. If one is permitted to liken the Sufites' dialectical theory to that of Hegel, Ibn Khaldun can be likened to Marx. Ibn Khaldun believed that society, as well as nature, is ruled by the dialectical process; but he seemed to see in the Sufite dialectic too much spiritualism or idealism to be rightly applied to the actual process of society. Ibn Khaldun took the Sufite dialectic, as Marx long after took that of Hegel, and "stood it on its feet"; that is, he took the Sufite theory, deprived it of its spiritualistic coloring, and fixed it anew upon a materialistic or sociologistic, basis.[8].

In arriving at his generalizations, Ibn Khaldun was relying on his own observations. During his lifetime, he witnessed several Islamic states that went through the process he described: their rise and fall. Even if Ibn Khaldun interpreted this cycle of history as an aimless, eternal recurrence of the same process that proves to be an application of the theory of a non-created and eternal world, it is basically unfamiliar to the Islamic mind. That is, the picture of history Ibn Khaldun drew is not the same as that of the theological view of history offered by revealed religions.[9] Since Ibn Khaldun's views represent his time, one can now observe the inability of the nomads and the ruralites to invade modern civilization (urban areas). Civilization is today no longer an abode of submissive people, as Ibn Khaldun claimed. (See Chapter 4.)

One can still raise the question: Can one consider Ibn Khaldun's ideas and explanations of the rise and fall of states a theory? This leads one to define the term *theory*. If theory is defined as a generalization concerning observed phenomena that is scientifically or systematically established, then Ibn Khaldun, to a large extent, was successful in forming a theory of the state based on the dynamic element or criterion of *asabiyah*. His comparative survey of seven centuries of Muslim life enabled him to note the rise and fall of governments,[10] especially in North Africa. He specifically noted the similarities in different places and different times. However, this theory is limited in scope; it may not be applicable to other regions of the world or even to other periods of time. In the field of sociology and in other related social sciences, many such theories are found. Of course, a theory that has a relationship to empirical sociolcultural realities can be amended, refined, and at a given time in history may even be rejected.

Is Ibn Khaldun a pessimist thinker? The question as to whether the Khaldunian cyclical theory is pessimistic has attracted many writers, some of whom characterized Ibn Khaldun as being a "pessimist" whose "history is purposeless," and hence whose ideas are "sceptical." He has also been characterized as a "fatalist," and a nonbeliever in progress.[11] This is not the case.

1. *Pessimism* is a natural impression to the reader of *The Muqaddimah*, but it is a false impression; the cyclical pattern is endless, and at first sight it offers little solace to man's ego. The solace is real, however, precisely because Ibn Khaldun refuses to concern himself with the ultimates of origins and ends. It is necessary only to say that all is from God and serves his purpose,"[12] which is to guide people to the straight (right) path.

2. Ibn Khaldun's ideas are causal. His view of the world is one of causal determinism, every phenomenon of social life is intelligible and understandable; it is determined by its causes.[13] Therefore, social phenomena can be understood and explained. Ibn Khaldun was not a fatalist.

3. Because Ibn Khaldun was concerned mainly with the political form of society (the state), a state's decline does not mean the end of the society itself. As has been shown, society is a going concern. (See Chapter 3.)

4. Ibn Khaldun's theory represents the actual events of his time: the stormy political life, the ups and downs of the states, the autocratic rule, and the corruptions of the leaders just before the state's fall.

5. Progress is a modern concept; it was, therefore, foreign to the medieval Muslims.[14]

6. Ibn Khaldun, like Comte, did not ignore the material

aspects of civilization. For Ibn Khaldun, this is the inevitable result of urbanization and urbanism.

7. Ibn Khaldun observed the moral consequences of the fall of the state, the return to the nomadic life with its emphasis on folkways, mores, and traditions – a "refinement" of the urban way of life as he saw it.[15]

8. Ibn Khaldun greatly emphasized cooperation and social solidarity as positive aspects of social organization and a stable government.

Is Ibn Khaldun a conflict theorist? Ibn Khaldun's ideas, especially in relation to the rise and fall of states, encouraged writers to place him "among the conflict theorists," especially because he emphasized causal principles in history at a time when providential viewpoints everywhere held sway.[6] Ibn Khaldun is also considered among the "outstanding early representatives" of social Darwinism.[17] Jean Bodin is another representative. The most explicit and extreme of the social Darwinists is Gumplowicz whose theories were adopted and modified by Ward. "Another disciple of these conflict theorists is Oppenheimer, who . . . combined the earlier insights of Ibn Khaldun with theirs. [Oppenheimer] is the outstanding defender of the thesis that the state originates in and through the struggle of contending groups, primarily those constituted by tillers and by nomads."[18] Although Oppenheimer "has only praise for Ibn Khaldun," the German writer noted only those parts of Ibn Khaldun's work which fit into his agrarian reform program, as can be seen in his 1926 edition of *Der Staat.*[19]

It should be emphasized here that the dialectic Ibn Khaldun saw operating in history is nothing more than a historical generalization based on empirical observations. Accordingly, Ibn Khaldun did not make any special effort at developing a conflict theory as such. Competition, greed, monoply, power, struggle, and war are all social phenomena, natural and inevitable in human society. Society is dynamic and change is expected. Moreover, no indication is found that Ibn Khaldun favored war as a solution to social "progress." War and other forms of struggle or conflict are only means used by people to achieve something in life. War, political strife, and political corruption adversely affect the state and the tranquility of the society as a whole.

Thus, one should keep in mind that Ibn Khaldun advocated cooperation as a means of successful living, stability, and social harmony. "He insisted upon the necessity of homogeneity for the existence of a stable state with almost the emphasis of a Giddings, and small wonder when one considers the similarity between *asabiyah* . . . and 'consciousness of kind.'"[20] One can agree therefore, with Lacoste[21] that one of Ibn Khaldun's major aspirations or wishes was to see a strong, firmly established, and stable state.

Is Ibn Khaldun a functionalist? The desire, aspiration, and need of an individual like Ibn Khaldun to see a stable government does not necessarily make that individual a functionalist. Although stability, "integration," and "equilibrium" are emphasized by functionalists, *functionalism* may be defined so broadly that it can actually cover many types of human relationships. Furthermore, functional and dialectical sociology are not mutually exclusive methodological approaches, but differ as to the level of critique on which they operate.

Ibn Khaldun and Other Social Thinkers

Ibn Khaldun is not the only thinker who dealt with the rise and fall of civilization. Polybius (205–123 B.C.) dealt with the cyclical nature of the historical process. His ideas were not known to Ibn Khaldun.[22] St. Augustine too saw the cycle of human history "from God to God . . . from Earthly paradise to Heavenly Paradise via the Fall and Redemption . . . a cycle completed only by members of the City of God, the chosen few."[23] Augustine's and Islamic thoughts are similar on the creation and on the concept of God as absolutely omniscient and omnipotent, but Ibn Khaldun was more realistic in his thinking. "Ibn Khaldun's cycle theory, while it somewhat resembled earlier cycle theories, was much more effectively developed."[24] Other thinkers also believed in a "pattern," "successive stages," or "periods" in the rise and fall of "states," "cultures," or "civilizations."

Vico, for instance, contended that every nation or culture passes through the same stages: "rise, development, maturity, decline, and fall."[25] In his words:

> Men first feel necessity, then look for utility, next attended to comfort, still later amuse themselves with pleasure, thence grow dissolute in luxury, and finally go mad and waste their substance.
> The nature of peoples is first crude, then severe, then benign, then delicate, finally dissolute.[26]

The essence of this quotation is that Vico and Ibn Khaldun believed that the urban way of life weakens people becaue of its emphasis upon leisure, luxury, and "vices," which make them liars, tricksters, and cowards.[27] Vico's remedy, the return to barbarism, means that a culture must evolve again through the same cycle,[28] or as Ibn Khaldun put it, the return to nomadism and the rise of a state through a new and strong *asabiyah*. Both thinkers emphasized the importance of religion and political leadership as factors in the development of human society. Religion provides a sense of belongingness or cohesion to the society. Vico's idea that "if a powerful man is to become monarch the people must take his side,"[29] corresponds to Ibn Khaldun's belief that any man who holds power deserves to be obeyed and respected. The man of power, according to Ibn Khaldun, may act unjustly sometimes, but this is not enough to counterbalance the social advantage that results from a power relationship. Men of power are the main factors behind social control. Without them, injustice becomes more prevalent.[30] Ibn Khaldun's idea is in accordance with his realistic thinking, which advocates that good and evil are two necessary aspects of one reality. Generally, neither he nor Vico believed that injustice and tyranny would endure.

Turgot's Combat Cycle also shows how history passes through periods of slow and rapid social change which succeed each other. The following passage from Turgot's work shows resemblance to Ibn Khaldun's thought; that is, barbarous people have sometimes overrun other peoples with a more complex culture and adapted to this culture:

The barbarians thus become civilized, more rich, more tranquil, more accustomed to a life of ease, or to say the least, a sedentary life, and therefore they soon lose the vigor which make them conquerors unless a saving discipline puts a stop to the inroads of luxurious sloth. If not, the conquerors yield to new barbarians, the domain becomes still more extensive, the new conquerors have their age of vigor and of decadence in turn, but even their fall helps to perfect the arts and ameliorate the laws.[31]

Marx's idea of history may be considered cyclical. He conceived of society's passing through successive evolutionary stages, from primitive communism (which Engels discussed at length in his *Origin of the Family*), to the slave system (in ancient Greece and Rome), to feudalism (in Ibn Khaldun's era, the period of the great clash between town and country), to capitalism, and to Communism. A return to the beginning is at a higher level of development.[32]

Marx and Ibn Khaldun both set forth a conception of historical change characterized by conflict and one which is dialectical in nature. Each successive stage arises from the conflicting contradictions of the previous one. Although Ibn Khaldun's conception of change is the cyclical rise and fall of dynasties in contrast to the more evolutionary postulates of Marx, to both these men these changes in stages are essentially dialectical. Their statements are congruent with one another. Because of his appearance in the nineteenth century, Marx was confident to say that "the history of all hitherto existing society has been the history of the class struggle."[33] Ibn Khaldun was more circumscribed in limiting his notion of conflict to one between the desert people and those in urban areas. Their dialectic does not rest on a reified metaphysical principle, but it is rooted in actual historic relations. *Historical materialism* is a better term to use than *dialectical materialism*, but this term can also be misleading in the light of the dialectical relationship between productive and nonproductive factors in history.[34] Confusion exists over this because when one abstracts from particular historical events and posits the dialectic as a scientific reality, it often seems as if it has been made into a hypostesized reality. One should remember Marx's admonition that "in direct contrast to German philosophy which descends from heaven to earth, here we ascend from earth to heaven."[35]

Gumplowicz held that the historic process is the record of the rise and fall of countless successive civilizations. He shared with Karl Marx the notion that change precedes primarily through a conflict of basic interests, which historically can be defined.[36] This process of conflict, Gumplowicz concluded, brings with it economic exploitation. As can be seen, this idea is similar to Ibn Khaldun's. Another striking similarity (to *asabiyah*) is shown in Gumplowicz's belief that no state has ever arisen except through the conquest of one group by another. Thus, "the minority of conquerors were able, in the first instance, to overcome, and later to exploit, the conquered majority because of superior unity and discipline, for unity and discipline are chief sources of the strength of all social groups.[37]

In *The Decline of the West*, Spengler viewed human history as a rise and fall of "cultures." Each culture passes through stages of childhood, youth, manhood (maturity), and old age (end). From this viewpoint Sarton considered Ibn Khaldun a forerunner of Spengler.[38] According to Spengler, civilization is the final stage, it is "a conclusion . . . . Death following life, rigidity following expansion";[39] it is marked by cosmopolitan lifestyle instead of folk relations, by science and money values instead of religion and traditional group values, and by sex instead of motherhood.[40] Civilizations may continue to survive for long periods, and may even revive, and have an "Indian summer." However, finally they lose the desire to be. Before its death, the civilization experiences a spell of second religiousity, a "fever of new religious movement, a wave of mysticism or gnosticism."[41] This is actually what happened in the last stage of Islamic civilization, as exemplified in the Sufism.

Living in the twentieth century, Spengler failed to make a clear distinction among the terms *civilization, culture,* and *society*. Generally, his writing style lacks a sociological touch.

For Sorokin, human culture begins with the "ideational" stage, which is unified and integrated around "the same supreme principle of true reality and value . . . a unified system of culture based upon the principle of a supersensory and superrational God as the true reality and value . . . ."[42] This is characteristic of the Western medieval era as well as the Brahman Indian, Buddist, and Taoist cultures. The emergence of a new idea, "namely, that the true reality and value is sensory" causes the decline of the ideational stage, corresponds to the materialistic and scientific perspective of reality: What is real is what one can perceive through one's senses. Because culture may not immediately move toward this direction, a combination of the sensory (empirical) and the supersensory results in a stage Sorokin called "idealistic." For Western culture, the idealistic stage corresponds to the thirteenth and fourteenth centuries, *e.g.,* Thomas Aquinas's efforts to combine the ideational Biblical view and the empiricism of Aristotelian philosophy. According to Cairns, "Sorokin supports his thesis by an examination of all the aspects of a great culture: the fine arts, sciences, philosophy and religion, ethics and law, social organizations and relations."[43] Sorokin concluded that no one absolute system of truth is found. The rhythmic cycle of truth is found in every one of these three cultures; thus, one finds repetition *as a new culture arises out of the old.* This rhythmic cycle proves that there cannot be "only one valid system of truth."[44] These ideas may refute Sorokin's insistence that his "theory of social and cultural change" is not cyclical.[45] Moreover, he did not specify why any one stage or phase of culture becomes predominant in any given era.[46] Sorokin's ideas clearly diverge from those of Ibn Khaldun, but his "very general vision of the impermanence of the things" is shared with the Arab thinker who stated that: "the world of the elements and all it contains comes into being and decays. This applies to both its essences and its conditions."[47] Ibn Khaldun believed that "duration belongs to God alone,"[48] and that "this entire world is trifling and futile. It ends in death and annihilation."[49] Unlike Ibn Khaldun's writing, one can detect a religious (Christian-Oriental) touch in Sorokin's discussion of the three stages of culture. This is also true of Toynbee's stages of cultural development.

Toynbee believed in the cyclical pattern of the rise and fall of great civilizations, although this is not without some "linear progress," specifically in religion. This cyclic pattern consists of four stages or periods: origin, growth, breakdown, and disintegration. "Each stage has peculiar characteristics that distinguish it from the others and provide a principle of interpretation by which to judge the contribution of each civilization."[50] Toynbee emphasized the process of challenge-and-response. When primitive people "met the challenge of a peculiarly difficult situation with a response of a peculiarly creative and successful sort, the civilization appeared."[51] Hence, the new stage of the growth of civilization. The second stage develops because of continuous challenge.[52] Some individuals in society possess "superhuman" qualities that enable them to initiate the process of growth. These creative personalities follow the process of withdrawal-and-return. "They must withdraw from the field of action of society in order to make their achievement of inspiration or discovery and then they must return to the field of action in order to try to convert the society to the new way of life they have envisioned."[53] When further challenges are not produced, civilization fails to continue to grow; its growth stops. This leads to the loss of creativity by the creative minority and loss of social solidarity. The way now is provided for the final stage, the disintegration of civilization, which is characterized by increasing divisions in both social and spiritual life, by "time of troubles," and by hostility between the majority and the minority. If the minority uses force to oppress the majority, the latter reacts against the minority by consolidating its forces and finding fulfillment in the creation of a universal church. The peoples outside the civilization in question organize themselves into "barbarian war bands" who attack and raid the citadels of the state until it falls.[54] For Toynbee, religion, specifically Christianity, is the real solution and hope for the salvation of human civilization. Thus exists a definite goal for the rise and fall of civilization, *i.e.*, the Kingdom of God. As can be seen, Toynbee and Ibn Khaldun found internal weaknesses and internal dissension as signs of breakdown of civilization. Both agreed that during the process of disintegration, the minority becomes a tyrannous clique, promoting, to a great extent, their own interests, "squeezing all the tax money possible out of the masses of the people for war and satisfaction of luxurious tastes."[55] This description fits not only Toynbee's and Ibn Khaldun's but also Vico's view of a declining civilization.[56]

Of all the theoretical explanations of the rise and decline of civilizations (cultures, states), Spengler seems far more extreme than Ibn Khaldun and others, *i.e.*, Spengler's "method is not as objective" as are those of the other thinkers.[57] Moreover, when Ibn Khaldun's ideas are compared with Vico's, Spengler's, Sorokin's, and Toynbee's thoughts, they seem to be, as Cairns puts it, "astonishingly modern."[58]

Ibn Khaldun, Vico, and Spengler agreed that "royal authority," monarchy, or "Caesarism" develop first out of equalitarian or democratic societies. According to Ibn Khaldun, Gumplowicz, and Toynbee, a minority of conquerors with unity, zealous, and discipline take over and exploit the conquered majority, a situation that leads to the eventual decline or fall of the civilization or state. The views of Ibn Khaldun, Vico, Gumplowicz, and Spengler on "progress" are seen by some writers as "pessimistic." Ibn Khaldun's and Spengler's conclusions also are regarded as "fatalistic." Ibn Khaldun, Vico, Sorokin, and Toynbee, like St. Augustine, stressed the significance of the Divine. They thought of religious faith as "the most potent factor in integrating a large civilization and in stimulating its creative growth."[59] Toynbee was especially more influenced by Christianity. In his work, *A Study of History*, Toynbee reaffirmed St. Augustine's views[60] by advancing a mystical and apocalyptic perspective.

Limitations or shortcomings are found in the works of all the writers who dealt with the rise and fall of civilizations or states. Ibn Khaldun is no exception. The limitation placed on his work is, in the words of Toynbee, "the axiom that all historical thought is inevitably relative to the particular circumstances of the thinker's own time and place."[61] The same can be said of others when we observe the failure of many of their predictions to come true.

In spite of its weaknesses, the Khaldunian cyclical theory deals with the development of human society. It does not necessarily seek the best possible state form; it emphasizes the up-and-down movement that develops and completes itself not into something higher and better, but into something different comprising the old and the new simultaneously. Hence, Ibn Khaldun's model is not static, because it deals with the eternal circulation of elites.[62]

Despite the shortcomings of the theories of the rise and fall of states or civilizations, they constitute an obviously valiant effort to make history a sociological science.[63] Furthermore, these theories serve a practical purpose: no state, regardless of how autocratic or brutal it might be, would endure. The social dialectic is always in operation. It ensures that social injustice, when it appears, does not persist.

Chapter 7

URBANIZATION AND URBANISM AS A MODE OF LIFE

This chapter treats the city as having and maintaining a way of thinking and behaving that is distinctly different from that of the rural and nomadic life. It shows that urbanism (as a way of life) is dependent upon urbanization, which is mainly ecological and demographic in nature. The relationships between social organization of the city, population increase, and the consequent population pressures and problems are discussed. The shortcomings of Ibn Khaldun's generalizations are mentioned, and his theoretical contributions are compared with those of other thinkers, especially Louis Wirth.

I. Urbanization

Urbanization (*tamaddun*) is an expected social phenomenon; it is the goal of *badw* (nomadic and rural people) who aspire to lead a life of ease, tranquility, and luxury. These people, or any conquerors for that matter, need not build a new city or a capital for themselves; they can retain any city used by the old dynasty. Often, however, establishing a state *may* mean establishing a city, *e.g.*, Baghdad at the beginning of the Abbasid rule and Cairo after the Fatimid invasion of Egypt.[1] Establishing a city marks the first stage of its existence, youthfulness. The second stage is maturity, followed by the stage of senility. Although Ibn Khaldun did not mention an "infantile stage," his ideas of the city's evolution are similar to those of Griffith Taylor.[2] However, in their discussions of the several factors contributing to urban evolution, Ibn Khaldun placed more emphasis on the social dimension; the city to him is a social phenomenon.

Requirements for Town Planning

According to Ibn Khaldun, in order to establish towns as places for dwelling and shelter, useful and necessary features should be introduced, "and all the conveniences . . . made available."[3] The following are the specific requirements:[4] (1) "The town should be situated in an accessible place, either upon a rugged hill or surrounded by a sea or by a river, so that it can be reached only be crossing some sort of bridge," thereby making an enemy overtaking difficult. (2) The air or the atmosphere should be safe from illness. It "is confirmed by direct observation that towns where no attention is paid to good air, have, as a rule, much illness." (3) Adequate transportation facilities, such as a river or a sea, are necessary to import essential and useful things. (4) Springs with plenty of fresh water are needed. (5) "Good pastures for the livestock of the inhabitants" must be provided. (6) Near the residential areas there should be some fields suitable for cultivation. Ibn Khaldun realized that these requirements "differ in importance according to the different needs and the necessity that exists for them on the part of the inhabitants."[5] In Ibn Khaldun's time, and in some places until a few decades ago, these requirements were essential for building a town. Today, a town need not be situated in an inaccessible area in order to defend itself, and a good pasture need not be near a town.

Moreover, Ibn Khaldun emphasized that the "construction" of cities cannot be achieved except through the following:[6] (1) "united effort"; (2) a great number of workers (when the state is large and farflung, "workers are brought together from all regions, and their labor is employed in a common effort."); (3) cooperation of the workers and craftsmen; (4) the use of machines, which may be needed to "multiply the power and strength needed to carry the loads required in building"; and (5) "engineering skill." Many people are unaware of the importance of machines and pulleys and engineering skill. "Many a travelled person can confirm what we have stated from his own observation of building activities and of the use of mechanics to transport building materials."[7] Ibn Khaldun believed that the reasons for the comparatively few buildings and construction in Islam were: (1) the Arabs in the beginning of their civilization, were nomadic and unfamiliar with the crafts; (2) Islam's forbidding the Arabs "to do any excessive building or to waste too much money on building activities for no purpose;" and (3) paying "little attention in town planning to making the right choice with regard to the site of the town, the quality of the air, the water, the fields, and the pastures belonging to it."[8] Ibn Khaldun cited the Arabs' planning of Kufah and Basra. "All they looked for when planning those cities was pasturage for their camels and nearness to the desert and the caravan routes. Thus, those cities do not possess a [preferred] natural site. They had no sources from which to feed their civilization (population) later on."[9] Ibn Khaldun erred here. Specifically, Basra is now the second largest city in Iraq, possessing an important natural site with a plentiful supply of water.

Size and Density

Not all cities are alike; they differ in size.[10] A city's size is, according to Ibn Khaldun, determined by a variety of factors, the most important of which is migration. Reasons for migration include: (1) the conquest and the subsequent settlement of the conquerors in the city; (2) luxury, which encourages people to "move to a city"; (3) the satisfaction of human needs by utilizing many facilities which the city provides;[11] (4) economic pull, for the city economy is an index to city size; and (5) the dependence of people on the "support and protection of a powerful state"[12] whose capital is usually an urban area.

Ibn Khaldun asserted that when the social organization of a city grows, its inhabitants increase in number.[13] This high man-to-land ratio means that the city has to take into account the needs of its inhabitants, especially if they "live in very crowded conditions." This is because people compete with each other for space. They also have differences over "things," such as "right-of-way and about outlets for running water and about refuse disposed of through subterranean conduits."[14] Here, Ibn Khaldun's ideas on the relationship between social organization of the city, population increase, and the consequent population pressure and problems are not too different from those described by classical and recent social scientists including demographers. Generally, his ideas on size, density, and heterogeneity of urban population are close to Durkheim's social morphology and Wirth's "theory of urbanism," as will be seen.

Ibn Khaldun pointed out that population increase indicates that the city will have to extend farther to include areas previously not utilized for living.

> ... The town will extend farther and farther. Eventually, the layout of the town will cover a wide area, and the town will extend so far and wide as to be almost beyond measurement. This happened in Baghdad and similar cities . . . .
>
> Baghdad included over forty of the adjacent neighboring towns and cities. It was not just one town surrounded by one wall. Its population was much too large for that. The same was the case with al-Qayrawan, Cordoba, and al-Mahdiyah in Islamic times. It is the case with . . . Cairo at this time, so we are told.[15]

This discussion of the growth of large cities such as Baghdad is similar to what is referred to today as the process of suburbanization.

Ibn Khaldun also mentioned several factors contributing to the decline of urban population. These factors include (1) coercion of the subjects by "bad government," which occurs primarily when revenues decrease; (2) numerous "famines," particularly when people under a "bad government" refrain from cultivating the soil; and (3) plagues, mainly as a result of the polluted air through too large a population.[16]

II. Urbanism as a Way of Life

This phrase is borrowed from Louis Wirth's famous 1938 article, of the same name.[17] Ever since that time, Wirth's presentation has been a point of departure for many of the discussions of the sociology of urban life.

For Ibn Khaldun, the "city is large and densely populated and unlimited in the variety of its conditions."[18] As a result, coordination of urban activities is indispensable. "The activities of the inhabitants of a city necessitate each other."[19] Some of the activities are "required for the necessities of life," and the others are "required for luxury customs and conditions" existing in highly developed urban areas.[20]

When a city's population grows, an increase in both labor and number of craftsmen should follow.[21] "As a consequence, industry and crafts thrive. The income and the expenditure of the city increase."[22] Affluence comes to those who work and produce things by their labor, which they may not even need.[23] The more numerous and the more abundant the urban population, the more luxurious their lives in comparison with those of the inhabitants of smaller urban areas.[24]

Demand for luxuries means also the refinement and development of crafts. Crafts "give elegance to all the various kinds of luxury."[25] For Ibn Khaldun, even the planting of fruitless trees of any kind in urban setting was a sign of extreme luxury, thereby indicating the nation's approaching decline. (The tree is an indication rather than a cause of the destruction of civilization).[26] He provided us with another interesting example of excessive luxury, of how beggars in a large city are better off than beggars in a small urban area. In Fez (Morocco), "I saw them beg for many kinds of luxuries and delicacies . . . . If a beggar were to ask for such things in Oran [Algeria], he would be considered with disapproval and treated harshly and chased away."[27]

Because of the luxury and tranquility he enjoys, the urban person becomes too weak to take care of his needs personally. He becomes dependent upon a protective force to defend him. Moreover, "luxury corrupts the character" and the religion of the urbanite.[28]

Immorality, wrongdoing, insincerity, and trickery, for the purposes of making a living in a proper or an improper manner, increase among [the urbanites]. People are now devoted to lying, gambling, cheating, fraud, theft, perjury, and usury. Because of the many desires and pleasures resulting from luxury, they are found to know everything about the ways and means of immorality; they talk openly about it and its causes, and give up all restraint in discussing it, even among relatives and close female relations . . . .

The city, then, teems with low people of blameworthy character. They encounter competition from many members of the younger generation of the dynasty, whose education has been neglected and whom the dynasty has neglected to accept. They, therefore, adopt the qualities of their environment and company, even though they may be people of noble descent and ancestry. Men are human beings and as such resemble one another. They differ in merit and are distinguished by their character, by their acquisition of virtues and avoidance of vices. The person who is strongly colored by any kind of vice and whose good character is corrupted, is not helped by his good descent and fine origin.[29]

Furthermore, sexual deviant behavior is also a consequence of urbanism and a cause for the decline of the civilization. Ibn Khaldun said:

Among the things that corrupt sedentary culture, there is the . . . diversification of the pleasures of sex through various ways of sexual intercourse, such as adultery and homosexuality. This leads to destruction of the human species. It may come about indirectly, through the confusion concerning one's descent caused by adultery. Nobody knows his own son, since he is illegitimate and since the sperm of different men got mixed up in the womb. The natural compassion a man feels for his children and his feeling of responsibility for them is lost. Thus, they perish, and this leads to the end of the human species. Or, the destruction of the human species may come about directly, as is the case with homosexuality, which leads directly to the non-existence of offspring.[30]

To summarize, division of labor and specialization not only provide people with a sense of cooperation and experience, but also make them more sophisticated in their urban way of life. The urbanites' sophisticated mode of life includes what Ibn Khaldun called "a particular code of manners in everything they undertake and do or do not do." Such mannerism is found in their ways of making a living and handling their customary affairs and their dealings with other people.[31]

The urban dwellers' lifestyle is the consequence of wealth and prosperity; and these, in turn, are the consequences of the urban mode of life. One leads to the other, until "confused conditions of city life," corruption, excessive luxury, weakening of religious influence, disappearance of the *asabiyah*, and reliance on strangers (clients) for protection work together to destroy the city.[32]

Ibn Khaldun's ideas are not without shortcomings:

1. A discrepancy seems to exist between his negative characterization of urban life and his statements that "much good can fully exist only in conjunction with the existence of some little evil."[33]

2. His emphasis on luxury as the main cause of a civilization's decline may be seen as an overexaggeration, even though he observed the decline of several states that enjoyed luxury. Moreover, the characteristics he attributed to urbanites, *e.g.*, "immorality," "wrongdoing," "insecurity," "trickery," and devotion to "lying," "gambling," "cheating," "fraud," and "theft," constitute a sweeping generalization. Not all urbanites, including Ibn Khaldun himself, have to devote themselves to these types of deviant behavior. The association between luxury and the creation of these forms of deviant behavior is neither clear nor convincing. Only after the association between the decline of religion as a form of social control and the increase of deviance in urban areas was made did Ibn Khaldun provide a convincing explanation.

3. Urbanism brings with it a positive contribution: an emphasis on learning leading to the development of arts and sciences. Ibn Khaldun himself admitted that "scientific instruction became firmly rooted"[34] in the city, and that when "the cities of Islam grew . . . illiteracy disappeared from among the Arabs because of their constant occupation with *The Koran*."[35] Thus, sciences such as "alchemy" and medicine exist and are numerous only when "sedentary culture" is "highly developed."[36]

Arithmetic, for instance, is indispensable to urban life, especially its application to business dealings. These sciences provide the urban inhabitants with knowledge, experience, and, as Ibn Khaldun stated, "intelligence."[37]

4. *Asabiyah* is not confined to tribal life of nomadic people. It is normally weak, but not absent, in the urban setting. It may take the form of coordination between people and their activities and institutions in the city, such as the economic institution. *Asabiyah* and its many ramifications cannot totally disappear unless the city, including its inhabitants, is completely destroyed.

5. The well-known and the most venerated mosques were, and still are, located in major cities: Mecca, Medina, and Jerusalem. Why would such large and significant mosques be built in urban areas? If they are needed to guide urbanites to the right "path," is it not an indication that religious influence is not disappearing and that religion may even thrive in the city? Religious sites in urban areas seem to increase as population size increases. Luxury and deviant behavior exist; but urban life, including religion, is a going concern.

Ibn Khaldun and Other Writers

City life has been a major concern of many thinkers including Ibn Khaldun. In Islam, al-Farabi's work on city life *al-Medina al-Fadilah*, was a utopia, and hence is speculative and subjective. A similar attempt to study city life was made by Ikhwan al-Safa in their *Rasa'il*.[38] Although city life has been equated by several writers with disorganization, corruption, immorality, and vice, these negative characteristics can also be a part of village life. By the same token, the positive qualities attributed to rural life may be found in the city.

Urbanism is considered a "protean" term. Customarily, it is used to denote a set or sets of qualities possessed by a large aggregation or settlement.[39] Ibn Khaldun saw the city as a natural stage in the development of human history; its growth, prosperity, and decline are aspects of his cyclical theory. The qualities he attributed to the urbanites is caused mainly by luxury which, in turn, is the result of the decline of *asabiyah* or social solidarity. Ibn Khaldun was not alone in his thinking concerning city life. Nearly three centuries after Ibn Khaldun's death, Vico made some similar statements about urban life especially in relation to luxury:

> Since peoples so far corrupted have already became naturally slaves of their unrestrained passions – of luxury, effeminacy, avarice, envy, pride, and vanity – and in pursuit of the pleasures of their dissolute life are falling back into all the vices characteristic of the most abject slaves (having become liars, tricksters, calumniators, thieves, cowards, and pretenders), providence decrees that they become slaves by the natural law of . . . nations . . . and that they become subject to better nations which, having conquered them by arms, preserve them as subject provinces. Herein two great lights of natural order shine forth. First, that he who cannot govern himself must let himself be governed by another who can. Second, that the world is always governed by those who are naturally fittest.[40]

Like Ibn Khaldun, Vico maintained that after fulfilling the necessity of life urbanites attend to comfort, pleasure, and luxury. "Vico agrees entirely with his remarkable predecessor, Ibn Khaldun, that sedentary culture weakens man because of its emphasis upon comfortable and then luxurious living with its pleasures and then dissolute living."[41]

In his *Division of Labor in Society*, Durkheim came close to Ibn Khaldun's notion of luxury, which includes art:

> [Art] is a luxury and an acquirement which it is perhaps lovely to possess, but which is not obligatory; what is superfluous does not impose itself. On the other hand, morality is the least indispensable, the strictly necessary, the daily bread without which societies cannot exist. Art responds to our need of pursuing an activity without end, for the pleasure of the pursuit, whereas morality compels us to follow a determinate path to a definite end. Whatever is obligatory is at the same time constraining.[42]

Another example of such similarities is provided by Strong. The city to him is materialistic. "As the city grows more prosperous and rich, the administration of its interests affords increased opportunities for corruption."[43] In fact, a variety of recently published data based on sound research confirms Ibn Khaldun's "observation that urban residence is associated with deviance from traditional values."[44]

Wirth's definition of the city and his three criteria of urbanism (size, density, and heterogeneity) had been stated six centuries earlier by Ibn Khaldun. To Ibn Khaldun *hadara* (equivalent to urbanism) is a way of behaving, a mode of social life similar to secularization.[45] Ibn Khaldun's lines of demarcation between urbanization as a process and urbanism as a way of life are much clearer than are those in Wirth's article. Moreover, Wirth's popular criteria of urbanism are not unique. For example, Durkheim, Weber, and Simmel had advanced similar ideas. Specifically, Durkheim's views on social differentiation in relation to size of population parallel those of Wirth and Ibn Khaldun. Recognizing the social significance of a community's population growth, Weber also made a statement similar to that of Wirth. According to Weber, "from a sociological point of view large numbers of inhabitants and density of settlement mean that the personal mutual acquaintanceship between the inhabitants which ordinarily inheres in a neighborhood is lacking."[46] Weber realized that "cultural factors play a role in the point where impersonality makes it appearance in human affairs." Unlike Simmel, he was unwilling to confine social analysis to the delineation of interpsychic form. In Simmel's, as well as in Spencer's, Wirth's, and Ibn Khaldun's studies, one finds that the focal point is "the urban mentality." To Simmel, "there is perhaps no psychic phenomenon which has been so unconditionally reserved to the metropolis as has the blasé attitudes."[47] This same observation was also made in one way or another by several writers including Ibn Khaldun, Durkheim,[48] and Wirth.[49] Simmel, moreover, emphasized another factor, the money economy, which dominates the metropolis and which becomes the common denominator of all values.[50] Again this observation is not too different from those made by several writers including Spengler,[51] Oppenheimer,[52] Wirth,[53] and Ibn Khaldun.[54]

Neither Simmel, nor Wirth, nor Ibn Khaldun used any sophisticated empirical methodology. Their data were based mainly on observation. Simmel was aware of the effort of the Industrial Revolution in the growth of European cities, including Berlin whose population by 1890 had increased tremendously.[55] Wirth observed many technological and scientific changes which affected the American city. And Ibn Khaldun witnessed the growth and problems of many cities, especially in North Africa. Even though based on observation, the ideas of these men cannot be fully accepted. Wirth's social heterogeneity as a criterion of urbanism is not clearly defined and cannot be easily applied crossculturally, especially to traditional societies. Several studies on the Third World show no evidence that city life tends to weaken the lineage or leads to the instability and insecurity Wirth suggested are the results of heterogeneity.[56] The migrant's family life remained stable, and extended family ties are emphasized and in some cases increased rather than decreased.[57] The migrants usually concentrate in a few specific localities where they maintain their traditions, ethnocentric behavior, and attitudes.[58] Similarly, Ibn Khaldun's views on luxury as a major cause of the corruption of the city and hence the decline of civilization are, at times, exaggerated.

Simon stated that according to Ibn Khaldun "the urbanites have no family in the proper sense."[59] Actually, unlike Wirth and some other recent social thinkers, Ibn Khaldun did not write about the declining social significance of the family.[60] In Ibn Khaldun's *Muqaddimah*, the family as a social institution received almost a total silence, an indication that it was not afflicted with "insecurity," "instabliity," or "disorganization." The old (tribal) ties may weaken, but they are replaced by similar ties. As he stated: "Many inhabitants of cities come into close contact through intermarriage. This draws them together and, eventually, they constitute individual related groups. The same friendship or hostility that is found among tribes and families, is found among them, and they split into parties and groups."[61]

It seems then that in light of this information about urban life, generalizing on urbanism as a way of thinking and behaving is more difficult than generalizing on urbanization as a process.

Chapter 8

THE KHALDUNIAN TYPOLOGY

In this chapter, Ibn Khaldun's analysis of *badawa* and *hadara* as a typology, and as a line of writing unfamiliar to many writers before him, is presented in detail. This typology is then briefly compared with other types, mainly of Tönnies, Durkheim, Redfield, and Becker.

I. Ibn Khaldun's *Badawa* and *Hadara*

Ibn Khaldun classified human social organization into two types: *badawa* (primitive life) and *hadara* (civilized life or urbanism). *Badawa*, however, is not a precise term and may even be considered inadequate. Literally, it means desert life or nomadic culture; but the Khaldunian term includes both the desert people and the inhabitants of the backwoods villages and other small rural communities. Inhabitants of these small communities "adopt the natural manner of making a living, namely agricultural and animal husbandry," as well as travelling around in order to find pasture and water for their animals.[1] To use Ibn Khaldun's terminology, hereinafter these desert-rural inhabitants will be referred to as *badw* (a term derived from *badawa*).

Both *badawa* (nomadism-ruralism) and *hadara*(urbanism) are natural social phenomena. "Differences of condition among people are the result of the different ways in which they make their living."[2] These two types may be compared in some detail as follows:

1. *Badawa* is the cradle of civilization and preceded sedentary life. Urban areas are indebted to *badawa* for the continuous flow of nomadic and rural population; "most" of the inhabitants of any given city originated among people "dwelling in the country and villages of the vicinity."[3] After enjoying city comfort and luxury, the *hadar* (urbanites) have no desire for desert or rural conditions, "unless they are motivated by some urgent necessity or cannot keep up with their fellow city dwellers."[4]

2. The population size is smaller in the area covered by *badawa*, and the density is lower, than that of *hadara*. This is mainly a result of the continuous movement from nonurban areas to the cities. Hence, the city is not only large and thickly populated but also unlimited in the variety of its attractive activities and conditions.[5]

3. Occupations in *badawa* are not as varied and complex as those of *hadara*. In *badawa*, agriculture and allied activities, such as animal husbandry, are the means of livelihood. Agriculture is the oldest of all crafts — it is prior to all other occupations and older than sedentary life itself, and all lives are dependent upon it.[6] Agriculture is a natural and simple procedure. "It needs no speculation or theoretical knowledge." As a rule, it is not practiced by urban population.[7] On the other hand, although large by number, urban "crafts" are secondary and subsequent to *badawa's* crafts.[8]

4. Specialization is more apparent in urban areas. Unlike the simple procedure of agriculture, the various urban occupations necessitate specialization and "perfection." They are "perfected" only if a large and perfect or well-developed sedentary civilization exists.[9]

5. People under *badawa* live less comfortably than do urbanites. The income of the *badw* "is not large, because they live where there is little demand for labor."[10] They usually experience a very hard time. "They obtain no more than the bare necessity, and sometimes less, and in no case enough for a comfortable or abundant life."[11] The urbanites, on the other hand, earn more and live more comfortably, i.e., beyond the level of bare necessity; and "their way of making a living corresponds to their wealth."[12] Because they live a life of abundance, the urbanites are not as healthy as the primitive *badw* and

therefore die more quickly than others, especially "when a drought or famine comes upon them."[13]

6. The primitive *badw* are more disposed to bravery than are urban people. The former "provide their own defense." This is not the case with city dwellers whose bravery decreases because of luxury, "laziness and ease," which lead them to entrust defense of their property and lives to others.[14]

7. Leadership is more democratic in *badawa*. However, the tribal leader who normally has humility in dealing with his men and respect for their feelings becomes highly insensitive to his group once he has established his rule in the city. He considers his men "despicable." He may even suppress the pride and vanity that arises in them after their victory over the urbanites. He becomes an absolute authority. As a result, his people may "revolt against him and despise him."[15] Luxury is responsible for driving a wedge between him and his group (or tribe). To use Pigors's terminology, his autocratic rule becomes "domination" rather than "leadership." As soon as "domination" begins to replace leadership in a state, the *asabiyah* gradually loses its vigor and binding force and eventually dies out.

8. *Asabiyah* is stronger among the *badw* people. This is because only groups or tribes held together by *asabiyah* can live in and near the desert. *Asabiyah* "produces the ability to defend oneself, to offer opposition, to protect oneself, and to press one's claims. Whoever loses *asabiyah* is too weak to do any of these things."[16] This also explains why the nomads are braver than the city dwellers. The nomads can dispense with the strong sense of solidarity after they settle down in the city, and eventually *asabiyah* "is altogether destroyed."[17]

9. Purity of lineage is found more explicitly in *badawa*. Here generations of primitive people grow up in the desert and backwoods villages; and, as a result, they become confirmed in their character and natural qualities. They do not mix with others. "Therefore, their pedigrees can be trusted not to have been mixed and corrupted. They have been preserved pure in unbroken lines." This characteristic is drastically different from that of the urbanites, whose lineages are "mixed up, and their groups intermingled." This is the case, for instance, with some early Arabs who acquired particular locations of residence after their conquest of many countries, including Spain.[18]

10. The *badw* are "closer to being good" and are less deviant than sedentary people. The nomadic "blameworthy qualities are much less numerous" than those of the urbanites who indulge in worldly desires. Many urban people "are found to use improper language in their gatherings as well as in the presence of their superiors and womenfolk. They are not deterred by any sense of restraint, because the bad custom of behaving openly in an improper manner in both words and deeds has taken hold of them."[19] The *badw* may be as concerned with worldly affairs as urbanized "civilized" people are, but their concern touches only the necessities of life.

It is the socialization process that is responsible for the prevalence of immorality, gambling, cheating, fraud, theft, and perjury in the city.[20] The same process is also responsible for preserving the "good qualities" of the *badw*.[21]

11. The *badw* are more religious than city dwellers. This is because, unlike the urbanites, the inhabitants of the desert and rural areas have accustomed themselves to hunger and to abstinence from pleasures. "The existence of pious men and ascetics" is, therefore, restricted to nonurban areas.[22]

12. The *badw* people are exposed to less change than are urban residents. In *badawa's* primitive setting, customs, manners, habits, and language persist in time.[23] Once the *badw* settle in urban areas, their cultural traits cannot and would not resist the pressure of city life. As their *asabiyah* declines, so do their traditions. Thus, social change is inevitable, especially in urban settings.

13. Formal social control is more conspicuous in the city. "Injustice and mutual aggression" are human qualities which are found in all human societies. Mutual aggression and mutual injustice of people in urban areas are averted by the influence of force and governmental authority "save such injustice as comes from the ruler himself."[24] The *badw* are not usually dominated by such formal social control. They are the most difficult people to rule. They tend to envy, rival dispute, and fight one another as soon as they are in proximity. When they see a sign of weakness in their leader, they quickly move to compete with him for the leadership.[25] Their only bond is their strong *asabiyah*, which is itself a restraining force with which to be reckoned. They are

subjected to the rules and traditions of the tribe as a whole and are expected to respect them.

14. Urbanites place more emphasis on education, arts, and sciences. Learning is stressed by city dwellers. The larger the urban area, the more emphasis on learning. When the Islamic cities grew, "illiteracy disappeared from among the Arabs."[26] Later, a great many colleges were built.

> As a consequence, mortmain endowments became numerous, and the income and profit from them increased. Students and teachers increased in numbers, because a large number of stipends became available from the endowments. People traveled to Egypt from Iraq and the Maghrib [Northwest Africa] in quest of knowledge. Thus, the sciences were very much in demand and greatly cultivated there.[27]

Moreover, arts and medicine are required only by sedentary culture. The *badw* do have a kind of medicine, but it is "mainly based upon individual experience."[28] People who grow up in villages and in civilized thinly populated areas cannot find scientific instructions even if they have "innate desire for scientific activity." Thus, sciences are greatly cultivated in the city. It is there where people become "widely versed in the various technical terminologies of scientific instruction, in the different kinds of sciences, and in posing problems and inventing new disciplines."[29] These scientific achievements become firmly rooted in sedentary culture. If civilization or the city fell, the scientific instruction ceased to be cultivated.[30]

Generally, the urbanites have more insight and are more clever than the *badw*. Sedentary culture contributes to "intelligence." This is especially so when the urbanites benefit from previous generations. "Good habits in scientific instruction, in the crafts," and in many other activities, "add insight to the intellect of a man and enlightenment to his thinking." One may, however, find bedouins whose understanding and intellectual capabilities are of the highest rank. "The seeming superiority of sedentary people is merely the result of a certain polish the crafts and scientific instruction gave them."[31]

Ibn Khaldun's Typology

Badawa	Hadara
1. Preceded *hadara*; it is the origin of civilization.	Indebted to *badawa* for its origin (population).
2. Small population with low density.	Large population with high density.
3. Occupations are limited mainly to agriculture and animal husbandry.	Occupations are varied but "secondary and subsequent" to *badawa's* crafts.
4. Division of labor and specialization are simple.	Complex division of labor necessitates specialization.
5. Bare necessities of living; less comfortable living.	Abundant and comfortable life.
6. More brave.	Less brave.
7. Democratic leadership.	Democratic rule declines in favor of autocracy.
8. Strong sense of solidarity (*asabiyah*).	Weak solidarity. *Asabiyah* may vanish.
9. Purity of lineage.	Pedigrees are "mixed up."
10. Closer to being good – "more remote from the evil habits."	More deviance and "blameworthy qualities."
11. More religious.	Less ready for divine worship.
12. Little or no change in customs and habits.	Change is inevitable and expected.
13. Emphasis is on informal social control.	Use of "restraining laws" by "authorities and the government."
14. Prevalence of illiteracy or minimal education.	Learning is stressed; arts and sciences are cultivated.
15. Generally, less clever.	More clever as a result of scientific and related activities.

Some of Ibn Khaldun's conclusions may not be applicable today. Some *badw* may be more "courageous" or "more brave" than some urbanites, but the entire urban population cannot be denied the characteristic of bravery. Moreover, urban areas are no longer subjected to nomadic military invasion. The urbanites are protected by a regular army and a police force and maybe even by zealous militiamen; it is the type of weapons, not physical strength, that provides more protection. Furthermore, contemporary nomadic people are subjected to central government laws and regulations; and from this view, they do not differ from the urbanites. Even in Ibn Khaldun's time, the nomadic people were dependent on the city in a variety of ways. As he stated, they "need the cities for their necessities of life."[32] They have "no hope of survival except by being obedient to the city. Thus, they are of necessity dominated by the urban population."[33]

As for the lifestyle, people under *badawa* still, generally speaking, live less comfortably than do the urbanites. However, today one witnesses the existence of many "urban" amenities in the deserts of, for example, Kuwait and Saudi Arabia. These amenities are made possible by the rapid cultural change including modern transportation facilities.

Concerning Ibn Khaldun's statement that the *badw* are "more religious" than the civilized urban dwellers, one may ask exactly how are they "more religious"? One is not given enough convincing evidence. The fact that they "have accustomed themselves to hunger and to abstinence from pleasures" does not necessarily make them "more religious." Moreover, "Islam is a predominantly urban religion which, arising first in the minds of town merchants, thoroughly reshaped the urban structures of the world it conquered."[34] As Benet puts it, "Islam was destined from the beginning to a predominantly urban history."[35] As noted before, the three most venerated mosques are located in the cities of Mecca, Medina, and Jerusalem.

Now a question may be raised: Did Ibn Khaldun favor *badawa*?

First of all, in Ibn Khaldun's opinion, the *badw*, especially nomads, are more capable than others of fighting and conquering other peoples. Man is naturally inclined to master others.[36]

A submissive man is imperfect, and yielding to humiliation of any kind indicates defectiveness in the essence of manhood. In this respect, the nomad is, in comparison to the urban person, superior.[37] Moreover, unlike the urbanite, the nomad normally does not evade social (tribal) control, and he refrains from cheating, gambling, adultery, fraud, usury, and similar behaviors. He, furthermore, does not have to emphasize commerce and craftsmanship that necessarily requires cunning and deception.[38]

However, Ibn Khaldun was in fact quite aware of the existence of certain "bad" traits among the nomads. He had distinguished himself from other students of the nomadic culture by viewing these bad traits as inherent by-products of good traits.[39] In other words, he did not view them as dichotomies in which absolute good is set against absolute evil; rather, he arranged social phenomena along a continuum. Living four years among nomadic people Ibn Khaldun found them poor, "more brave," and stronger than urban people; but they were nevertheless, less obedient to the rules of an orderly life.[40] They also had (at the time of Ibn Khaldun) a profound contempt for sciences and for intellectual learning,[41] in spite of the fact that there was a deep-rooted inclination in Islam toward all scientific endeavors. According to Islamic Traditionalists, Muhammad urged his followers to seek scientific knowledge.

II. Relation to Other Typologies

Among social thinkers, especially sociologists, classifying social organizations or human societies into two main types is in vogue. For example, Spencer classified them into militant and industrial; Maine, status and contract; Tönnies, *Gemeinschaft* and *Gesellschaft*; Durkheim, mechanically solidary and organically solidary; Ogburn, stationary and changing; Sorokin, unibonded and multibonded; Redfield, folk and urban; and Becker, sacred and secular. This task has also been accomplished by, for instance, Confucius, Plato, Aristotle, St. Augustine, St. Thomas Aquinas, and Ibn Khaldun.

For the sake of brevity, the typologies of Tönnies, Durkheim, Redfield, and Becker will be emphasized and compared with Ibn Khaldun's types.

Ibn Khaldun's typology of *badawa* and *hadara* and to a large extent those of others, *e.g.*, Sorokin, Redfield, Becker, and Durkheim, constitute a "system of value judgement which contains the old Rousseauan notion of primitive people as noble savages, and the corollary that with civilization has come the fall of man."[42] For Ibn Khaldun, he was able to explain the reason behind the dialectical process in human history through the polarization of the two value systems.

Generally, in discussing rural-urban typologies, the term urban (or civilization) has come to mean both differentiation and disorganization. However, Becker's objection to this loose usage of the term urban is understandable. Social disorganization exists also in nonurban areas. Even Becker's "sacred society" may not escape change that results in social disorganization. Sociologists widely differ in their opinions regarding the main factor behind the secularization process in the sacred society. It is considered to be the growth of popuation and the rise of division of labor (Durkheim); trade and commerce (Tönnies); the introduction of technology and scientific knowledge (Veblen); conflict and war (Gumplowicz); cultural contact and communication (Becker); the dialectical process of sociocultural dynamics (Sorokin); and so on. It is perhaps permissible to conclude that a sacred society can be secularized by any one or more of these factors.

At age thirty-two, Tönnies published his *Gemeinschaft und Gesellschaft*, described by Rudolf Heberle as a "profound and beautiful treatise . . . which marked a turning point in the history of sociology."[43] The first edition of this work appeared at a time when, generally speaking, sociology was identified with Herbert Spencer's evolutionary theory of history which Heberle described as "historically naive and politically inconsistent."[44] In addition to the fact that "in *Gemeinschaft und Gesellschaft* Tönnies has especially acknowledged the decisive stimulus which he received from Sir Henry Maine's antithesis of status and contract,"[45] some of Tönnies's ideas are similar to those of Ibn Khaldun.

Both Ibn Khaldun and Tönnies were influenced, in their writings, by their experiences and observations. Ibn Khaldun witnessed the growth and development of some cities in North Africa and southern Spain. He also visited several nomadic tribes and lived among one of them for about four years. On the other hand, Tönnies himself went through the process of assimilation "from a social background predominated by 'community' values and norms to a social milieu of essentially 'associational' type," when, as a young man, he left a countryside of farms and small towns for the world of big cities.[46] Chambliss pointed out that Tönnies's typology represents "a good example of a later attempt to analyze the same basic situation that claimed the attention of Ibn Khaldun more than five centuries ago."[47] For instance, Tönnies's description of the house (as an entity in itself) in the village and in the town,[48] is similar to Ibn Khaldun's description of the economic conditions of badawa and hadara. In both Gemeinschaft and badawa, springs, wells, and streams may be used as community property;[49] and in both, one can see a common religion, a common code of custom and mentality, a common dialect, and a common set of material culture traits, e.g., types of houses, dress, and furniture.[50]

Social solidarity also is an important factor in determining the connection between badawa and mechanically solidary society on the one hand, and hadara and organically solidary society on the other. In badawa and mechanically solidary society, the totality of beliefs and sentiments are common to all members;[51] homogeneity of individual morals and traditions are expected. The more primitive communities are, the more resemblances are found among their members.[52] Such resemblances link the individual with his group. People oppose any attack, especially from the outsiders, and the reaction, consequently, is general and collective.[53] A crime against such people is considered an offense against their moral sentiments, punishable by repressive mores.[54] In hadara and organically solidary society, complex division of labor and specialization stimulate differentiation and "contractual relations." People here are hetergeneous mentally and morally. As a result, weakening of the "collective conscience" and asabiyah is expected.[55] Ibn Khaldun's generalization concerning the well-developed division of labor in urban areas, as a result of change from one way of life (*badawa*) to another (*hadara*), comes close to Durkheim's idea on the rise of the division of labor as a result of the shift from mechanical solidarity to organic solidarity. Both Ibn Khaldun and Durkheim agreed that material "progress" in *hadara* and in organically solidary society does not necessarily make people "any happier." To Ibn Khaldun, more contentment is usually found in primitive *badw* society where people are devout and very religious.

Durkheim's description of mechanical and organic solidarity might have been inspired, to some extent, by North African ethnographic material; the same area which Ibn Khaldun had studied some five centuries earlier. Gellner makes an affirmative statement in this regard: "The ethnographic material on which this crucial dichtomy is based is of course primarily North African."[56] At any rate, Durkheim's description of industrial societies is, of course, based on his own experience of them.

Redfield's characteristics of the folk society are clearly similar to those of Ibn Khaldun's *badawa*. Both folk society and *badawa* are small, isolated, nonliterate, and homogenous. Both also have and maintain a strong sense of solidarity. Division of labor and technology are simple; behavior is traditional; and kinship ties are of great significance in life.

Becker's sacred and secular societies have several things in common with Redfield's and Ibn Khaldun's typologies. The characteristics of the sacred society are, generally, similar to those of the folk society and *badawa*. As for the secular society and *hadara*, both are vicinally, socially, and mentally accessible; and in both tradition and ritual are minimal; rationality is predominant; change is expected, and offense against the laws invokes little social disapproval.[57] Sacred and secular types are considered a variation of Tönnies's *Gemeinschaft* and *Gesellschaft* types of organized social system. Sorokin believed that "Becker's theory hardly represents an improvement on the – somewhat similar – theories of St. Augustine, Vico, Ibn Khaldun," or even his own.[58]

In Ibn Khaldun's *badawa* and *hadara*, in the *Gemeinschaft* and *Gesellschaft* as described by Tönnies, in the mechanical and organic societies of Durkheim, in the presentation by Maine of status society and contract society, in the sacred-to-secular conceptualization of Becker, and in the folk-urban contrast of Redfield, there exists the underlying assumption of social and cultural transformation. In such typologies, man is seen as moving from a relatively simple, undifferentiated network of relationships, largely based upon primary relationships, strong in tradition and in emotional bonds, toward the opposite conditions.

Chapter 9

SUMMARY
AND CONCLUSION

Many Western sociologists believe that sociology began with
Comte who coined the term *sociology*, which is a combination
of Latin and Greek, science of society. The objective of this
book is to demonstrate and to maintain that Ibn Khaldun first
laid the foundations of what came to be called sociology. He
was well convinced of the uniqueness of his work, which he
named *ilm al-umran* (science of social organization).[1] Some of his
ideas are pertinent to the nature, scope, and methods of
sociology. Briefly:

1. Society is a reality, *sui generis*, an idea similar to that of
Durkheim. The two thinkers saw the group as an entity apart
from the individuals, and both agreed that self-preservation of
human society cannot be achieved except through "social
organization," cooperation, and social unity.[2]

2. Human society can be considered the subject matter of
Ibn Khaldun's new independent science. It is however mean-
ingless to study society apart from *asabiyah* (social solidarity).

3. *Asabiyah*, as a driving force in the development and
growth of human society, is an index of the strength, stability,
and cohesiveness of society. Ibn Khaldun assigned a similar
significance to *asabiyah* as Durkheim did to *conscience collective*.
Asabiyah may lose its vigor if tyranny replaces democratic
leadership in a state.

4. Ibn Khaldun, like Comte, treated polity from the
historical and analytical points of view and differentiated

between theocracy and sociopolitical phenomena. They made it clear that a well-defined division of labor is inevitable for the development and growth of the state, a point which has been greatly emphasized by Durkheim.

5. Ibn Khaldun described and analyzed the history of every stage of state, its rise, development, maturity, decline, and fall. Vico, Turgot, Marx, Gumplowicz, Brooks Adams, Spengler, Sorokin, and Toynbee also conceived of civilization, culture, or state as passing through definite stages from the simple, traditional, religious, sacred, or nomadic, to a rational, secular, or urban entity where disorganization and disintegration occur. Ibn Khaldun's ideas in this regard are considered "astonishingly modern."[3]

6. Human society has a culture which is learned and shared. Strong norms and for this matter any other restraining influence or social control are needed to regulate social interaction. This idea is similar to that of Vico, Comte, Durkheim, and others who have indicated that human society is a very important and powerful monitor of human conduct. Ibn Khaldun and Comte, for instance, did not rule out the possibility of using force as a means of social control to keep society stable and integrated.

7. Ibn Khaldun made a clear distinction between urbanization as a process and urbanism as a way of life. He anticipated Wirth's definition of the city and his criteria of urbanism.[4] In addition to his emphasis on population size as an index of specialization and division of labor,[5] Ibn Khaldun, like Durkheim, Simmel, Spengler, and Wirth, dealt with the urban mentality and heterogeneous social interaction.

8. Ibn Khaldun compared city life with nonurban culture. His typology of *badawa* (nomadism-ruralism) and *hadara* (urbanism) is especially similar to Tönnies's *Gemeinschaft* and *Gesellschaft*, and to Maine's status and contract. These typologies, like those of Redfield (folk-urban), Sorokin (familistic-contractual), and Durkheim (mechanical solidarity-organic solidarity), represent a system of value judgments, showing simple primitive rural people as noble beings and sophisticated (civilized) urban people as suffering from "impersonal," "secular," and "immoral" conditions that may lead to their

downfall. Discussing the development of typologies from Confucius to contemporary social scientists, Sorokin concluded that Ibn Khaldun's analysis of *badawa* and *hadara* "is one of the most penetrating, detailed, and enlightening."[6]

9. Ibn Khaldun stated that "differences of condition among people are the result of the different ways in which they make their living."[7] This should not be interpreted to mean that he is an economic determinist.[8] Ibn Khaldun gave a predominant, but not exclusive, position to the economic factor in history. His detailed analysis of the significance of the economy for the functioning of human society does not mean that he neglected the noneconomic factors such as *asabiyah* and religion. He, like Durkheim and recent sociologists, considered religion a social phenomenon, culturally determined. Human society, therefore, can exist and persist without "religious laws." Ibn Khaldun preceded Durkheim, Malinowski, and others in emphasizing the positive role of religion as a means of social control and in maintaining group solidarity. His analysis of religion as an important social factor is considered "the beginning of a sociology of religion."[9]

10. Ibn Khaldun showed great interest in natural laws; an interest which later was perpetuated by Vico, Comte, Durkheim, Tönnies, and others. Ibn Khaldun was abe to discover and to lay down the law of causality in his study of social organization.

11. Explicitly or implicitly, the major characteristics of science are found in his *Muqaddimah*; his writings are based on careful observation; they are also theoretical, cumulative, and objective. His aim was to describe and analyze human society rather than to discover remedies for its ills. Contemporary sociology emphasizes this point, especially in basic sociological research.

12. Ibn Khaldun's methods, which consist of comprehensive observation, use of historical documents, and comparison, are the very methods used by the "pioneers" of sociology and "masters" of social theory. Neither Comte, nor Simmel, nor Tönnies, nor Weber, nor the hundreds of early sociologists used any "sophisticated" empirical methodology; their data were based mainly on their own observations.[10] Quantification has only

recently received attention from sociologists. Even today, many of the findings in sociology, ethnology, and related disciplines are based on qualitative methods.

The fact that Ibn Khaldun's observation was mainly in North Africa does not make his writing nonsystematic or nonobjective. Durkheim made "boldest generalizations on the slim basis of his theory-laden view of one very particular religion"[11] in central Australia. In fact, many recent sociological studies are based on observation of one specific community or locality group.

13. Ibn Khaldun was aware that societal conditions do not change in the same manner. His theory, like those of many sociologists, does not explain all aspects of social change.

14. If a personal (antagonistic) feeling toward urban life is detected in his writing this is not unique in the social sciences. Sociology, for example, endeavors to avoid value judgment, but "sociologists have sometimes failed to control their personal feelings, beliefs, and values, with the result that biases have not been uncommon in sociological work."[12]

Ibn Khaldun then was a realistic thinker and not a philosopher. He was not satisfied with philosophy and its logical deductions which frequently did not correspond to his actual observations of human social organization and social change. Like Vico and Comte, Ibn Khaldun's basic thesis dealt with the interpretation of history in terms of social change. Ibn Khaldun is considered a philosopher of history, a historiographer, whose social or sociological interpretation of history was developed by Vico, Turgot, Condorcet, Comte, and even Spencer. This theme has important implications for social theory. As C. Wright Mills argued, "the general problem of a theory of history cannot be separated from the general problem of a theory of social structure."[13] However, history is still construed by some to be an ideographic discipline which differs from sociology, a nomothetic discipline.[14] This tends to justify, with a few notable exceptions,[15] mutually exclusive scholarship within two separate disciplines. A solution to the dilemma of how to preserve sociology as a generalizing science taking into account historical variations *in society* is suggested in Ibn Khaldun's work. In his writings, one can find a dialectical synthesis between history and what is now known as sociology, which incorporated the aspects of *change*. Dialectical means that his approach to the study of human social activity resembles that of, for instance, Marx, *i.e.*, to grasp things and their images, ideas, essentially in their interconnections.[16]

The question arises: What is the lesson we can learn from studying the theory of a fourteenth-century thinker? Some writers believe that it is more useful to concentrate on studying and understanding the latest theories since they are the end-products of the creative works of the past. Such an argument may be valid in the natural sciences, but in the social sciences, the newer generalizations may not be more valid than the old ones. Variations in social conditions and cultural backgrounds of people can influence the formation of social theories. Indeed, some of Ibn Khaldun's fourteenth-century generalizations may not be realized today. The nomadic people, including the Bedouins, are too weak to invade urban areas. Usually, they are controlled by laws and regulations of the urban central government. Due to the process of sedentarization of the nomads, the desert is now thinly populated. In addition, continuous migration of the ruralites to the urban centers may not weaken their *asabiyah*. The impact of the tribal life is strong even beyond the boundaries of *badawa*. Urban people in the Arab countries, specifically in the Gulf area, are still using their tribe's name as their surnames, and they are still proud of their nomadic customs, which they maintain and respect.[17] Despite the processes of sedentarization, industrialization, and modernization, and contrary to Ibn Khaldun's prediction, nomadic values and norms are still found in urban areas; they constitute an integral part of urban man's personality.[18]

Conversely, much of Ibn Khaldun's characterization of urban, especially political, life is still valid, *e.g.*, the luxury, tranquility, and involvement of some officials in commercial activities. His observation that tyranny normally leads to *ta'alluh* (egotism) on the part of the ruler is as conspicuous a phenomenon today as it was in Ibn Khaldun's time. If in Ibn Khaldun's time the ruling and the wealthy classes were able to immortalize their achievements by hiring individuals to record them in book form, today the mass media can likewise be used effectively by the ruling elites to glorify themselves and their accomplishments. Again, as in Ibn Khaldun's time, and as long as bullets take the place of ballots, the men of power seldom cede their positions or power to others.[19] If Ibn Khaldun were alive today, he might be somewhat amazed by the almost endless variety of urban "luxury"; but he would not be surprised to witness what he himself experienced in the fourteenth century: rivalries, plots, and upheavals as common features of political life. He might be pleased to see his political theory applicable even today. Thus, Ibn Khaldun's concept of *asabiyah* and its application to, and impact upon, nomadic-rural and urban ways of life constitute what can be called the Khaldunian sociological school of thought. Despite its shortcomings, and without minimizing the significanc of modern and contemporary sociology, this Khaldunian model can very well be utilized to study human society, its origin, growth, and development. The model is especially applicable to the societies of the Third World including the Arab countries.

A new science may be vague at the beginning.[20] Sociology is no exception. Ibn Khaldun was modest enough to admit his "imperfections," and was scientific enough to ask scholars to look at his work "with a critical, rather than a complacent eye."[21] The successors of a new science may gradually add more information "until the discipline is completely presented."[22] The post-Comtean phase of the development of sociology itself suffered from "imperfection" but, nevertheless, has been prolific, diversified, and differentiated.

Science is not a monopoly of any individual or any group. One can no longer insist that Auguste Comte is the founder of sociology when more and more evidence is found that Ibn Khaldun systematically discussed many of the main issues in the field of sociology. While several sociologists doubt the originality of Comte's work, believing that there is extremely little in his theoretical work that can be termed original, one finds that more and more sociologists and other social scientists agree that large portions of Ibn Khaldun's ideas are quite "modern" or relevant even today.

To reiterate, Ibn Khaldun himself was quite aware that he had discovered a science, *sui generis*, different from other sciences. Many of his ideas obviously anticipated both classical and modern sociological thought. Given the variety of concepts discussed, the theoretical orientation analyzed, and, above all, the time of his scholarship, Ibn Khaldun deserves to be studied not only as a pioneer but perhaps even as the founder of the generalizing science of sociology.

NOTES

Preface

1. Abdullah Shrait, *Al-Fikr al-Akhlaki ind Ibn Khaldun* (Tunis: The National Publishing Co., 1975), p. 209. A similar statement was also made by A. K. Ghallab, "al-Iltizam al-Ilmi ind Ibn Khaldun," *Mahrajan Ibn Khaldun* (Casablanca: Dar el-Kitab, 1962), p. 28. See also S. G. Shiber, "Ibn Khaldun: An Early Town Planner," *Middle East Forum*, Vol. 38 (March 1962), p. 35; M. A. Nashat, "Ibn Khaldoun: Pioneer Economist," *L'Egypte Contemporaine*, Vol. 35 (Cairo, 1945), p. 383; N. Schmidt, *Ibn Khaldun: Historian, Sociologist and Philosopher* (New York: Columbia University Prss, 1930), p. 45; A. J. Toynbee, *A Study of History* (New York: Oxford University Press, 1962), Vol. 3, p. 322.

2. P. von Sivers, "Back to Nature: The Agrarian Foundations of Society According to Ibn Khaldun," *Arabica*, Vol. 27 (February 1980), p. 89.

3. S. Faghirzadeh, *Sociology of Sociology* (Tehran: Soroush Press, 1982).

4. Ibn Khaldun, *The Muqaddimah: An Introduction to History*, trans. by Franz Rosenthal (Princeton: Princeton University Press, 1967), Vol. 1, p. 7.

5. See Chapter 2.

6. A. Comte, *The Positive Philosophy* (New York: AMS Press, 1974), pp. 51–398.

7. Quoted from S. Lukes, *Emile Durkheim: His Life and Work: A Historical and Critical Study* (New York: Penguin Books, 1973), pp. 82–83.

8. É. Durkheim, *The Rules of Sociological Method*, trans. by S. A. Solovay and J. H. Mueller (New York: The Free Press, 1938), p. lix; and H. E. Barnes, "Herbert Spencer and the Evolutionary Defense of Indi-

vidualism," in H. E. Barnes (ed.), *An Introduction to the History of Sociology* (Chicago: University of Chicago Press, 1948), p. 117.

9. R. Heberle, "The Sociology of Georg Simmel: The Forms of Social Interaction," in Barnes *Ibid.*, p. 249.

10. M. Weber, *From Max Weber: Essays in Sociology*, trans. by H. H. Gerth and C. Wright Mills (New York: Oxford University Press, 1946), p. 129.

Chapter 1

1. See A. J. Toynbee, *A Study of History* (New York: Oxford University Press, 1962), Vol. 3, p. 322.

2. M. A. Enan, *Ibn Khaldun: His Life and Work* (Lahore: Sh. Muhammad Ashraf, 1969), p. 65.

3. *Ibid.*, pp. 69–71.

4. See F. Baali and A. Wardi, *Ibn Khaldun and Islamic Thought-Styles: A Social Perspective* (Boston: G. K. Hall, 1981), pp. 20–21; Enan, *op. cit.*, p. 21; T. Hussein *Étude analytique et critique de philosophie sociale d'Ibn Khaldoun* (Paris: A. Pedone, 1917), p. 22.

5. N. Schmidt, *Ibn Khaldun: Historian, Sociologist and Philosopher* (New York: Columbia University Press, 1930), p. 43.

6. See Enan, *op. cit.*, pp. 69–71.

7. O. G. von Wesendonk, "Ibn Chaldun, ein arabischer Kulturhistoriker de 14 Jahrhunderts," *Deutsche Rundschau*, Vol. 49 (1923). See the Arabic translation by M. A. Enan in Hussein's Arabic edition of *Étude analytique et critique de la philosophie sociale d'Ibn Khaldoun*, pp. 175–176.

8. S. al-Husri, *Dirasat an Muqaddimat Ibn Khaldun* (Beirut: Kashshaf Press, 1943), p. 65.

9. For more details on Ibn Khaldun's work, See F. Rosenthal's lengthy and comprehensive introduction to his translation of Ibn Khaldun's *The Muqaddimah: An Introduction to History* (Princeton: Princeton University Press, 1967), pp. lxviii–cxv; Schmidt, *op. cit.*; P. K. Hitti, *Makers of Arab History* (New York: St. Martin's Press, 1968), pp. 238–256; M. A. Enan, *op. cit.*; and H. Simon, *Ibn Khalduns Wissenschaft von der Menschlichen Kultur* (Leipzig, 1959), pp. 29–38.

10. See K. Mannheim, *Ideology and Utopia* (New York: Harcourt, Brace, 1936), Ch. 5, *passim*.

11. *Ibid.*, p. 270. See also G. de Gré, *Society and Ideology: An Inquiry into the Sociology of Knowledge* (New York: Columbia University Bookstore, 1943), p. 98.

12. Hussein, *op. cit.*, p. 28; Enan, *op. cit.*, pp. 186–187.

13. Ibn Khaldun, *The Muqaddimah: An Introduction to History*, trans. from the Arabic by F. Rosenthal (Princeton: Princeton University Press, 1967), Vol. 1, p. 252, and *passim*. Hereinafter, this translation will be referred to as IK–FR, followed by volume number (in Roman numerals) and pagination (in Arabic numerals). Excerpts reprinted with permission from Princeton University Press.

14. IK–FR, I:282–283, 306; IK–FR, II: 295–296; and *passim*. See also A. Wardi, "Ibn Khaldun wa al-Mujtama al-Arabi," *A'mal Mahrajan Ibn Khaldun–1962* (Cairo: National Center for Social Research, 1962), pp. 522, 523.

15. E. I. J. Rosenthal, "Ibn Khaldun: A North African Muslim Thinker of the Fourteenth Century," *Bulletin of the John Rylands Library*, Vol. 24 (1940), pp. 307–308.

16. See. T. B. Bottomore, "The Ideas of the Founding Fathers," *European Journal of Sociology*, Vol. 1 (1960), p. 33.

17. R. Walzer, "Aspects of Islamic Political Thought: Al-Farabi and Ibn Xaldun," *Oriens*, Vol. 16 (1963), p. 42.

18. M. Mahdi, *Ibn Khaldun's Philosophy of History* (Chicago: University of Chicago Press, 1964), pp. 33, 275, 285, 286. See also I. B. Madkoor, "Ibn Khaldun: al-Faylasoof," *A'mal Mahrajan Ibn Khaldun* (Cairo, 1962), pp. 124–125; M. A. al-Jabiri, *Al-Asabiyah wa al-Dawla* (Casablanca: Dar al-Thakafa, n.d.), pp. 149, 159–160.

19. Simon, *op. cit.*, pp. 11, 39, 45, 77.

20. IK–FR, III:246–251. Vico also criticized philosophers for failing to give certainty to their reasonings. See G. Vico, *The New Science*, trans. by T. G. Bergin and M. H. Fisch (Ithaca, N.Y.: Cornell University Press, 1968), p. 63, parag, 140; L. Pompa, "Vico's Science," *History and Theory*, Vol. 10 (1971), p. 54.

21. IK–FR, III:247.

22. IK–FR, III:257, 310.

23. IK–FR, III:254–257.

24. Baali and Wardi, *op. cit.*, p. 7. Later, Bodin also felt that instead of the Aristotelian logic an alternative technique was needed. See Jean Bodin, *The Six Bookes of a Commonweale*, ed. with introduction by K. D. McRae (Cambridge, Mass.: Harvard University Press, 1962), pp. A25–A26.

25. See. D. B. MacDonald, *The Religious Attitude and Life in Islam* (Chicago: University of Chicago Press, 1908), p. 131.

26. M. L. Jum'ah *Tarikh Falasifat al-Islam* (Cairo: Ma'arif Press, 1927), pp. 234–238; and Hussein *op. cit.*, p. 94.

27. T. J. de Boer, *The History of Philosophy in Islam* (New York: Dover Publications, 1967), pp. 188–189. A well-known controversy raged in Islam as a result of Ibn Rushd's hostility toward al-Ghazzali. In order to refute al-Ghazzali's work *Tahafut al-Falasifah* (Incoherence of Philosophers), Ibn Rushd wrote the *Tahafut al-Tahafut* (Incoherence of the Incoherence). The two books are now considered classics in Islam.

28. Baali and Wardi, *op. cit.*, p. 77.

29. Simon, *op. cit.*, p. 41.

30. *Ibid.*, p. 47.

31. *Ibid.*, p. 41.

32. See de Boer, *op. cit.*, p. 202; M. Fakhry, *A History of Islamic Philosophy* (New York: Columbia University Pres, 1970), p. 130; Bouthoul, op. cit., pp. 83–84, 85–86; M. M.Rabi' "Manhaj Ibn Khaldun," *L'Egypte Contemporaine*, (April 1970), 444; A. A. Isa, "Manhaj al-Bahth al-Ilmi ind Ibn Khaldun." *A'mal Mahrajan Ibn Khaldun* (Cairo, 1962), pp. 253–254, 257; M. A. al-Hababi, "Isalat al-Manhajiyah ind Ibn Khaldun," *Mahrajan Ibn Khaldun* (Casablanca: Dar el-Kitab, 1962), p. 13; A. A. Shrait, *Al-Fikr al-Akhlaki ind Ibn Khaldun (Tunis: Al-Sharika al-Wattaniya, 1975), pp. 59, 72; Enan, op. cit.*, pp. 126, 132–133. E. Rosenthal points out that Ibn Khaldun was "an empiricist, and thus averse to speculation . . . . His main interest centered round the group, the community of individuals organized in the State." E. I. J. Rosenthal, *op. cit.*, pp. 311, 312.

33. IK–FR, I:6, 15, 63, 71.

34. IK–FR, I:9.

35. P. A. Sorokin, *Society, Culture, and Personality* (New York: Cooper Square Publishers, 1962), p. 20; R. Flint, *History of the Philosophy of History* (New York: Charles Scribner's Sons, 1894), p. 158; H. E. Barnes, *A History of Historical Writing* (New York: Dover Publication, 1962), p. 96; Schmidt, *op. cit.*, 17; de Boer, *op. cit.*, pp. 204, 205; Simon, *op. cit.*, pp. 36, 141–142, W. M. Watt, *Islamic Political Thought — The Basic Concepts* (Edinburgh: The University Press, 1968), Vol. 6, p. 107; Enan, *op. cit.*, p. 160; Ignace-Abdo Khalife's introduction to Ibn Khaldun's *Sifa'us-Sa'-il Litahzib-il-Masa'il* (Beirut: The Catholic Press, 1959), p. 15.

36. IK–FR, I:6.

Chapter 2

1. See H. Becker and H. E. Barnes, *Social Thought from Lore to Science* (New York: Dover Publications, 1961), Vol. 2, pp. 565–566. The main proponents of this view are Gumplowicz, Sorokin, Becker, Barnes, and Chambliss.

2. L. von Wiese, *Systematic Sociology* (New York: Arno Press, 1974), p. 666. See also Becker and Barnes, *ibid.*, pp. 566–567.

3. Von Wiese, *ibid.*

4. N. S. Timasheff, *Sociological Theory: Its Nature and Growth* (New York: Random House, 1967), p. 25; Becker and Barnes, *op. cit.*, p. 498; R. W. Smith and F. W. Preston, *Sociology* (New York: St. Martin's Press, 1982), p. 9; R. Perrucci and D. D. Knudsen, *Sociology* (St. Paul, Minn.: West Publishing Co., 1983), p. 12; R. T. Schaefer and R. P. Lamm, *Sociology* (New York: McGraw-Hill, 1983), p. 512. D. Popenoe, *Sociology* (Englewood Cliffs, N.J.: Prentice-Hall, 1986), p. 9; and A. Thio, *Sociology: An Introduction* (New York: Harper and Row, 1986), p. 10.

5. A. Comte, *The Positive Philosophy*, trans. by H. Martineau (New York: Calvin Blanchard, 1855), p. 463 and *passim*.

6. Comte, *ibid.*, pp. 456, 469–471, and *passim*.

7. See Comte, *ibid.*, pp. 457, 462–464; P. A. Sorokin, *Society, Culture, and Personality* (New York: Cooper Square Publishers, 1962), p. 21; R. Chambliss, *Social Thought from Hammurabi to Comte* (New York: Dryden, 1954), pp. 401. 403.

8. A number of undocumented inferences from historical events can be detected in Comte's writings. Durkheim believed that "Comte identified historical development with the idea he had of it, which does not differ much from that of the layman." É. Durkheim, *The Rules of Sociological Method*, trans. by S. A. Solovay and J. H. Mueller (New York: The Free Press, 1938), p. 20.

9. Positivism is the third state of intellectual progress. Unlike the first two states, the theological and the metaphysical, the positivistic state is characterized by objectivity or scientific endeavors. A. R. J. Turgot envisaged Comte's "law" of the three states of human progress; it also was anticipated by M. Burdin. See Becker and Barnes, *op. cit.*, Vol. 2, pp. 472–473; 501–502.

10. See, for example, Becker and Barnes, op. cit., Vol. 2., pp. 575, 580, 679; H. E. Barnes, "The Social and Political Philosophy of Auguste Comte: Positivist Utopian and the Religion of Humanity," in H. E. Barnes (ed.), *An Introduction to the History of Sociology* (Chicago: University of Chicago Press, 1948), p. 88.

11. F. Tönnies, *On Social Ideas and Ideologies*, ed. and trans. by E. G. Jacoby (New York: Harper and Row, 1974), p. 92.

12. Durkheim, *op. cit.*, p. 29, also pp. 14, 143, 146. See also E. Durkheim, *Elementary Forms of Religious Life*, trans. by J. W. Swain (London: George Allen and Unwin, 1971), p. 18.

13. Comte, *Positive Philosophy*, pp. 444–446.

14. Some sociologists have repeatedly indicated that extremely little in Comte's theoretical work can be termed original. His major contribution was to provide systematic form to some of the somewhat incoherent doctrines current in his time. "As a matter of fact, Comte was greatly behind the scientific achievements of his age in many ways ... and quite failed to absorb many of the most important developments of the period which have since entered into sociological thought." Becker and Barnes, *op. cit.*, Vol. 2, p. 565; A. Aron, *Main Currents in Sociological Thought* (New York: Doubleday, 1968), Vol. 1, pp. 73, 117; S. Andreski, "Introduction" to A. Comte, *Essential Comte-Selected from Cours de Philosophie Positive*, trans. by M. Clarke (New York: Barnes and Nobles Books, 1974), p. 15.

15. F. Markham's introduction to Saint-Simon, *Social Organization, the Science of Man and Other Writings* (New York: Harper Torchbooks, 1964), p. xxxiii. See also D. D. Runes, *Dictionary of Philosophy* (Paterson, N.J.: Littlefield, Adams and Co., 1961), p. 275; T. B. Bottomore,

"The Ideas of the Founding Fathers," *European Journal of Sociology,* Vol. 1 (1960), pp. 35-36.

16. Andreski, *op. cit.,* pp. 9-10; Aron, *op. cit.,* pp. 13, 83.

17. É. Durkheim, *Montesquieu and Rousseau: Forerunners of Sociology* (Ann Arbor: The University of Michigan Press, 1970), pp. 1, 61.

18. J. D. Douglass and Associates, *Introduction to Sociology: Situations and Structures* (New York: The Free Press, 1973), pp. 27-28.

19. Sorokin, *op. cit.,* p. 20; Sorokin, *et al.* (eds.), *A Systematic Source Book in Rural Sociology* (Minneapolis: University of Minnesota Press, 1930). Vol. 1, p. 54; M. Mahdi, "Ibn Khaldun," *International Social Science Encyclopaedia* (New York: MacMillan, 1968), Vol. 7, p. 53. Although very briefly, Barnes and Sorokin were the first to introduce Ibn Khaldun's writings to the American reader.

20. See, for example, Sorokin *et al., op. cit.,* pp. 54-55; Sorokin, *op. cit.,* p. 20; N. Schmidt, *Ibn Khaldun: Historian, Sociologist and Philosopher* (New York: Columbia University Press, 1930), pp. 27-33; Becker and Barnes, *op. cit.,* Vol. 1, pp. 271-276; H. Z. Ülken, "Ibn Khaldoun, Initiateur de la sociologie," *A'mal Mahrajan Ibn Khaldun-1962* (Cairo: National Center for Social Research), p. 29; I. Lichtenstadter, *Islam and the Modern Age* (New York: Bookman Associates, 1958), p. 154; Chambliss, *op. cit.,* p. 312; T. B. Irving, "A Fourteenth-Century View of Language," in J. Kritzeck and R. B. Winder (ed.), *The World of Islam* (London: Macmillan, 1960), p. 185; M. A. Enan, *Ibn Khaldun: His Life and Work* (Lahore: Sh. Muhammad Ashraf, 1969), pp. 126, 132; M. A. Nashat, "Ibn Khaldoun: Pioneer Economist," *L'Egypt Contemporaine* (Cairo), Vol. 35 (1945), pp. 381, 383; Z. H. Pasha, "Ibn Khaldun, Sociologist: A Fourteenth Century Pioneer," *Actes du XV᷄ Congres International de Sociologie* (Istanbul, 1952), p. 85; M A. M. Nour, "An Analytical Study of the Sociological Thought of Ibn Khaldun," dissertation (Lexington: University of Kentucky, 1953), pp. 120-121: M. M. Rabi', *Political Theory of Ibn Khaldun* (Leiden: E. J. Brill, 1967), pp. 44, 47: F. Baali and A. Wardi, *Ibn Khaldun and Islamic Thought-Styles: A Social Perspective* (Boston: G. K. Hall, 1981), pp. vii, 7, 77-85; S. Al-Husri, "La sociologie d'Ibn Khaldoun," *Actes de XV᷄ Congres International de Sociologie* (Istanbul, 1952), pp. 285-291; G. Bouthoul, *Ibn Khaldoun: sa philosophie sociale d'Ibn Khaldoun* (Paris: 1930), pp. 29-38; A. A. Ezzat, *Ibn Khaldoun et sa science sociale* (Cairo: Universite de Fouad, 1947), pp. 55-63; O. Qudsi, "Ibn Khaldun ur Auguste Comte ka tkabla Mutala'a," unpublished manuscript, in Urdu, pp. 1, 7-10; M.

Behi, "Imamat Ibn Khaldun fi al-Ma'rifah," *A'mal Mahrajan Ibn Khaldun* – 1962 (Cairo: National Center for Social Research, 1962), pp. 418-419; H. Sa'ati, "Al-Manhaj al-Ilmi fi Muqaddimat Ibn Khaldun," *ibid.*, pp. 216-218; M. Fahmi, *Ilm al-Ijtima* (Cairo: I'timad Press, 1938), pp. 13-18; A. Wardi, *Mantiq Ibn Khaldun* (Cairo, 1962), chs. 12 and 13. According to Al-Khadhairi, "Most of the Arab writers in the first half of this century insisted that Ibn Khaldun is a sociologist. Why? Maybe an ethnocentric attitude which made those writers imagine that Ibn Khaldun's attempt was purely sociological." Zainab al-Khadairi, *Falsafat al-Tareekh ind Ibn Khaldun* (Cairo: Dar al-Thakaafa, 1979), p. 5. This statement contradicts another one in her book. On p. 82 she points out that "Ibn Khaldun is *the* founder of sociology." (Emphasis added.)

21. IK-FR, I:77.

22. *Ilm* means a science, but no precise translation exists for the term *al-umran*. It may mean "social organization," "civilization" (IK-FR, I:3; P. K. Hitti, *Makers of Arab History* [New York: Harper, 1968], p. 253), "human association" (Nour, *op. cit.*, p. 19; M. Mahdi, *Ibn Khaldun's Philosophy of History* [Chicago: University of Chicago Press], 1964, p. 87), "culture" (Mahdi, *ibid.*, *passim*; H. Simon, *Ibn Khalduns Wissenschaft von der Menschlichen Kultur* [Leipzig, 1959], p. 93; IK-FR, p. lxxx), "a social life" (S. Batsieva, *Al-Umran fi Muqaddimat Ibn Khaldun*, Arabic translation by R. Ibrahim [Tunis and Libya: Al-Dar al-Arabiya Lilkitab, 1978], p. 188), "population" (A. Schimmel, *Ibn Chaldun. Ausgewahlte Abschnitte aus der muqaddima* [Tubingen, 1951]. Although "social organization" and "civilization" come very close to the original term, the former wil be emphasized throughout this volume. Note, too, that this is the case of "sociology." Something of the growing pain of sociology is reflected in the definitions of the discipline. Sociologists broadly define sociology as the science of society. Other definitions cite the discipline's corpus as "social institutions," "social systems," "social action," "human relationships," "social processes," "social interaction," "social structure," "social groups," "social behavior," "collective behavior," "social phenomena," and the like. F. Baali and C. D. Bryant, *Introductory Sociology* (Chicago: Rand McNally, 1970), p. 2; F. Baali and M. C. Moore, "The Extended Deliberation: Definitions of Sociology," *Sociology and Social Research*, Vol. 56 (July 1972), p. 437; R. J. Pellegrin, "The Study of Social Change and Theory," *Sociological Spectrum*, Vol. 2 (July–December 1982), p. 223.

23. IK-FR, I:77-78, also I:84, 85.

24. IK-FR, I:78, also I:91.

25. IK-FR, I:78.

26. IK-FR, I:83. Ibn Khaldun believed that he "omitted nothing" concerning the nature, scope, "changes and variation" within social groups. "I treated everything comprehensively and exhaustively and explained the arguments for and causes of its existence." IK-FR, I:13.

27. IK-FR, III:481. Hence, Bouthoul's statement (*op. cit.*, p. 21) that Ibn Khaldun lacked modesty when discussing his new science, cannot be accepted. Ibn Khaldun's modesty is also clearly shown when he discussed his book's uniqueness: "I am conscious of imperfection . . . I confess my inability to penetrate so difficult a subject. I wish that men of scholarly competence and wide knowledge would look at the book with a critical rather than a complacent eye." IK-FR,, I:14. F. Rosenthal states that "in later Muslim scholarship, it was considered disrespectful to suggest that earlier scholars knew less than oneself or than other, more recent men." Footnote 19 in IK-FR, I:78. This may explain Ibn Khaldun's statement concerning his new science: "I do not know if this is because people have been unaware of it, but there is no reason to suspect them (of having been aware of it). Perhaps they have written exhaustively on this topic, and their work did not reach us." IK-FR, I:78.

28. IK-FR, I:10, also 11, 13, 71.

29. IK-FR, I:15, 79.

30. IK-FR, I:10, 65.

31. IK-FR, I:14, also 13, 56-57, 65.

32. See IK-FR,, I:71-72, 76-79, 80, 83; IK-FR, III:285-287, Hitti, *op. cit.*, p. 252; Simon, *op. cit.*, pp. 13, 38; Bouthoul, *op. cit.*, pp. 20-21; Hussein, *op. cit.* pp. 40-43; Becker and Barnes, *op. cit.*, Vol. 1, pp. 269, 277; A. Wardi, "Ibn Khaldun wa al-Mujtama al-Arabi," *A'mal Mahrajan Ibn Khaldun — 1962* (Cairo, 1962), p. 519; Hussein Fahim, *Qissat al-Anthropologia* (Kuwait, 1986), pp. 64, 68.

33. Charles Issawi, *An Arab Philosophy of History* (London: John Murray, 1950), pp. 7, 8, 36. See also Hitti, *op. cit.*, p. 252; Baali and Bryant, op. cit., p. 1; Simon, *op. cit.*, pp. 13, 38; Becker and Barnes, *op. cit.*, Vol. 1, p. 277; Bouthoul, *op. cit.*, pp. 20-21; Hussein, *op. cit.*, pp. 40-43; Wardi, "Ibn Khaldun wa-al-Mujtama al-Arabi," p. 519.

34. *Ibid.*

35. Schmidt, *op. cit.*, p. 21. See Hussein, *op. cit.*, p. 33.

36. Sorokin *et al.*, *op. cit.*, Vol. 1, p. 54; IK-FR, I:371; H. A. R. Gibb, "The Islamic Background of Ibn Khaldun's Political Theory," in S. J. Shaw and W. R. Polk (eds.), *Studies on the Civilization of Islam* (Boston: Beacon Press, 1962), p. 172; Rabi', *op. cit.*, p. 42; Simon, *op. cit.*, p. 121; T. J. de Boer, *The History of Philosophy in Islam* (New York: Dover Publications, 1967), p. 204; Nashat, *op. cit.*, p. 382.

37. H. V. White, "Ibn Khaldun in World Philosophy of History," *Comparative Studies in Society and History*, Vol. 2 (1959-1960), p. 114.

38. IK-FR, I:369, 371.

39. IK-FR, II:346.

40. Schmidt, *op. cit.*, pp. 20-27; Bouthoul, *op. cit.*, p. 16; Gibb. *op. cit.*, p. 167; Hussein, *op. cit.*, pp. 30-56, 161; Simon, *op. cit.*, p. 121; G. D. Cohen, "Ibn Khaldun: Rediscovered Arab Philosopher," *Midstream*, Vol. 5 (Summer, 1959), p. 81; Nour, *op. cit.*, p. 246; Ülken, *op. cit.*, pp. 32, 33, 35; de Boer, *op. cit.*, pp. 203-204.

41. See, for example, IK-FR, 1:12, 15-16, 177, 178, 179, 182, 183, 351, 366-367, 368, 370, 374, 376; IK-FR, II:204, 222, 223, 224, 225, 229, 239-240, 244-245, 246, 274, 335, 339; IK-FR, III:302, 371.

42. IK-FR, I:351.

43. IK-FR, II:244, 246.

44. See Hussein, *op. cit.*, p. 98; and Y. Lacoste, *Ibn Khaldoun: naissance de l'histoire passe du tiers monde*, Arabic translation by M. Sulaiman (Beirut: Ibn Khaldun House, 1973), p. 204.

45. *Op. cit.*, p. 250.

46. See, for example, IK-FR, I:11-13, 298; IK-FR, II:41-42, 268, IK-FR, III:361.

47. See, for example, IK-FR, I:66-67, 472-481; IK-FR, II:268. See also Enan, *op. cit.*, p. 136, de Boer, *op. cit.*, 206; Rabi', *op. cit.*, pp. 16, 41: and Ülken, *op. cit.*, p. 29.

48. W. J. Fischel, *Ibn Khaldun in Egypt: His Public Functions and Historical Research (1332-1406) — A Study in Islamic Historiography* (Berkely and Los Angeles: University of California Press, 1967), p. 119.

49. *Ibid.*, pp. 119-120.

50. *Op. cit.*, p. 247.

51. IK-FR, II:288.

52. IK-FR, II:290. See also de Boer, *op. cit.*, p. 206.

53. IK-FR, I:58, also 15–16, 56; IK-FR, II:6.

54. IK-FR, I:58.

55. IK-FR, I:368–369.

56. IK-FR, I:7.

57. IK-FR, I:7, 8, 9, 371.

58. IK-FR, I:72.

59. IK-FR, I:71–72; Baali and Wardi, *op. cit.*, pp. 105–107.

60. See E. I. J. Rosenthal, *Islam in the Modern National State* (Cambridge: Cambridge University Press, 1965), p. 26. See also IK-FR, I:408; IK-FR, II:418–420; IK-FR, III:281; Mahdi, *Ibn Khaldun's Philosophy of History,* p. 171; A. G. Widgery, *Interpretation of History: Confucius to Toynbee* (London: George Allen and Unwin, 1961); and H. K. Sherwani, *Studies in Muslim Political Thought and Administration* (Lahore: Sh. Muhammed Ashraf, 1959), pp. 213–214.

61. IK-FR, I:9.

62. IK-FR, II:429.

63. IK-FR, III:285.

64. IK-FR, III:285–286.

65. IK-FR, III:287.

66. IK-FR, I:76.

67. IK-FR, I:76–77.

68. Hussein, *op. cit.*, pp. 37–38.

69. Cited by A. J. Toynbee, *A Study of History* (New York: Oxford University Press, 1962), Vol. 3, p. 326. Fischel, *loc. cit.* Some writers raise the question as to whether the figures concerning taxes in Baghdad, Cairo, and other places, which Ibn Khaldun gathered might have been exaggerated. See IK-FR, I:361–368.

70. IK-FR,, I:6–8, 15–57, 71, 79, 83, 275–276, 290, 316–317, 369–370, 371; IK-FR, II:60, 87, 204–207, 209, 210, 213–214, 244–246, 324, 383; IK-FR, III:253.

71. Fischel, *op. cit.*, p. 113. See also A. K. Ghallab, "Al-Iltizam al-Ilmi ind Ibn Khaldun," *Mahrajan Ibn Khaldun* (Casablanca: Dar el-Kitab, 1962), p. 26. Unlike Vico, Ibn Khaldun was able to free himself from the fables and delusions. And unlike Jean Bodin (d. 1596), Ibn Khaldun did not believe "in the influence of the stars on the fortunes of individuals, nations, and states." See U. Farrukh, *The Arab Genius in Science and Philosophy*, trans. by J. B. Hardie (Washington, D. C.: The American Council of Learned Societies, 1954), pp. 132, 135.

72. See Gibb, *op. cit.*, p. 169; Mahdi, *Ibn Khaldun's Philosophy of History*, p. 293; Rabi', *op. cit.*, p. 31; M. M. Rabi', "Manhaj Ibn Khaldun fi ilm al-Umran," *L'Egypte Contemporaine* (Cairo, April 1970), p. 477; Chambliss, *op. cit.*, p. 312; Issawi, *op. cit.*, p. 13; Simon, *op. cit.*, p. 20; Ülken, *op. cit.*, p. 31; Lacoste, *op. cit.*, 75; M. al-Talibi "Nadariyat Ibn Khaldun fi Sultat al-Dawla," *al-Fikr* (Tunis, March 1961), p. 534.

73. B. Carra de Vaux, "Farabi," *Encyclopedia of Islam* (Leiden: Brill, 1927), Vol. 2, p. 54.

74. See al-Farabi, *Al-Madinah al-Fadilah* (Cairo: Nile Press, n.d.), p. 90.

75. Mahdi, *Ibn Khaldun's Philosophy of History*, p. 293.

76. Runes, *op. cit.*, pp. 89–90.

77. Durkheim, *op. cit.*, p. 15.

78. Bouthoul, *op. cit.*, p. 90.

79. *Ibid.*, p. 89.

80. See, for example, IK–FR, I:73; Hussein, *op. cit.*, p. 106.

81. Bouthoul, *op. cit.*, pp. 83, 84, 90.

82. See, for example, Becker and Barnes, *op. cit.*, Vol. 1, p. 269; de Boer, *op. cit.*, p. 203; Simon, *op. cit.*, p. 111; Chambliss, *op. cit.*, p. 295; M. A. al-Alim, "Muqaddimat Ibn Khaldun," *al-Fikr al-Arabi*, Vol. 1 (November–December 1978), p. 45.

83. IK–FR, I:77–78; Comte, *op. cit.*, pp. 399, 485, 486.

84. For more detail see Baali and Wardi, *op. cit.*

85. Schmidt, *op. cit.*, p. 45.

86. Durkheim, *The Rules of Sociological Method*, pp. xlv, xlvi; Durkheim, *Montesquieu and Rousseau*, pp. 63–64. Durkheim added: "The time has come for sociology . . . to assume the exacting character befitting every science." *The Rules of Sociological Method*, p. 146.

87. See Sorokin, *op. cit.*, p. 20.

88. Comte, *Positive Philosophy*, pp. 445-446, 484; Timasheff, *op. cit.*, p. 30.

89. Becker and Barnes, *op. cit.*, p. 269; Schmidt, *op. cit.*, p. 45.

90. Comte, *Positive Philosophy*, pp. 498, 508, and *passim*; Timasheff, *op. cit.*, p. 30.

91. IK-FR, I:249. See also IK-FR, I:250; IK-FR, II:316-319, 326-328, 356-357; IK-FR,III: 151-152.

92. Comte, *Positive Philosophy*, p. 515 and *passim*; Timasheff, *loc. cit.*

93. Schmidt, *op. cit.*, p. 29.

94. See Simon, *op. cit.*, pp. 36-37; Sati al-Husri, *Dirasat an Muqaddimat Ibn Khaldun* (Beirut: Kashshaf Press, 1943), p. 611.

95. Enan, *op. cit.*, pp. 150-152, 183; Hitti, *op. cit.*, p. 254.

96. Husri, *Dirasat*, pp. 612-613.

97. A. A. Ezzat, *"Tatawir al-Mujtama'a al-Bashari ind Ibn Khaldun,"* *A'mal Mahrajan Ibn Khaldun* (Cairo, 1962), pp. 52-53.

98. See Qudsi, *op. cit.*, pp. 8-9.

99. See IK-FR, III:286.

100. Timasheff, *op. cit.*, p. 29.

101. Vico, Montesquieu, and Quetelet are also considered the real predecessors of sociology. To some extent, this may be likened to the discovery of America. To many of us, Columbus is the "real" discoverer of America. To archaeologists, the American "Indians" have been in the continent for approximately 15,000 years!

102. See Chapter 3 and Chambliss, *op. cit.*, p. 312.

Chapter 3

1. See H. E. Barnes, "The Social Political Philosophy of Auguste Comte: Positivist Utopia and the Religion of Humanity," in H. E. Barnes (ed.), *An Introduction to the History of Sociology* (Chicago: University of Chicago Press, 1948), p. 85; H. E. Barnes "Herbert Spencer and the Evolutionary Defense of Individualism," in Barnes (ed.), *ibid., p. 135*; N. S. Timasheff, *Sociological Theory: Its Nature and Growth* (New York: Random House, 1967), pp. 183-184; N. J.

128   IBN KHALDUN'S SOCIOLOGICAL THOUGHT

Spykman, *The Social Theory of Georg Simmel* (New York: Atherton Press, 1966), pp. 32, 34.

2. É. Durkheim, *The Division of Labor in Society*, trans. by G. Simpson (New York: The Free Press, 1933), p. 339. "For Durkheim the word society has its roots in the Latin *communitas* rather than *societas*." R. A. Nisbet, *Émile Durkheim* (Englewood Cliff, N. J.: Prentice-Hall, 1965), p. 34.

3. IK–FR, I:89, 380, 389; IK–FR, II:137.

4. IK–FR, I:84.

5. E. I. J. Rosenthal, "Ibn Khaldun: A North African Muslim Thinker of the Fourteenth Century," *Bulletin of the John Rylands Library*, Vol. 24 (1940), pp. 308, 309. See also H. Simon, *Ibn Khalduns Wissenschaft von der Menschlichen Kultur* (Leipzig, 1959), pp. 64, 99; M. A. Enan, *Ibn Khaldun: His Life and Work* (Lahore: Sh. Muhammad Ashraf, 1969), pp. 154–156.

6. Including backwoods villagers.

7. See, for example, É. Durkheim, *Montesquieu and Rousseau: Forerunners of Sociology* (Ann Arbor: University of Michigan Press 1970), pp. 63–64; J. Willer, "The Implications of Durkheim's Philosophy of Science, "*Kansas Journal of Sociology*, Vol. 4 (Fall 1969), p. 176.

8. See S. Lukes. *Émile Durkheim — His Life and Work: A Historical and Critical Study* (New York: Penguin Books, 1973), p. 80.

9. E. Durkheim, *Elementary Forms of Religious Life*, trans. by J. W. Swain (London: George Allen and Unwin, 1971), p. 16. See also E. Benton-Smullyan, "The Sociologism of Émile Durkheim and His School," in Barnes (ed.), *op. cit.*, pp. 505, 506. Neither Durkheim nor Ibn Khaldun was "anti-individualistic." They were pro-society. On Durkheim's views see Willer, *loc. cit.*

10. Durkheim, *The Division of Labor in Society*, p. 96.

11. See H. Becker and H. E. Barnes, *Social Thought from Lore to Science* (New York: Dover Publications, 1961), Vol. 1, p. 277. Similar views were also expressed by T. Hussein, *Etude analytique et critique de la philosophie sociale d' Ibn Khaldoun* (Paris: A. Pedone, 1917), p. 58; sati al-Husri, *Dirasat an Muqaddimat Ibn Khaldun* (Beirut: Dar al-Kashshaf, 1943), p. 236; Simon, *op. cit.*, pp. 23, 121; Enan, *op. cit.*, p. 122; T. B. Irving, "A Fourteenth-Century View of Language," in J.

Kritzeck and R. B. Winder (eds.), *The World of Islam* (London: Macmillan, 1960), p. 185.

12. IK-FR, I:374-375.

13. *Ibid.*

14. C. H. Cooley, *Social Organization* (New York: Charles Scribner's Sons, 1909), p. 23.

15. R. Heberle, "Preface," in F. Tönnies, *Gemeinschaft and Gesellschaft*, English trans. (East Lansing, Mich.: Michigan State University Press, 1957), p. x.

16. IK-FR, I:389.

17. IK-FR, I:90, 276-277, 284-285, 331.

18. IK-FR, I:473.

19. IK-FR, I:390.

20. IK-FR, II:137-138.

21. IK-FR, I:391, also 269, 390.

22. IK-FR, II:3.

23. IK-FR, II:271-272, also 4.

24. A. Comte, *The Positive Philosophy* (New York: Calvin Blanchard, 1855), pp. 510-511 and *passim*; Becker and Barnes, *op. cit.*, Vol. 2, p. 710.

25. Durkheim, *The Division of Labor in Society*, p. 364.

26. *Ibid.*, pp. 397, 407.

27. IK-FR, I:90, 380, also 79, 89, 91, 356, 358. IK-FR, II:417, also 241.

28. Durkheim, *The Division of Labor in Society*, p. 399.

29. See F. Baali, *Falsafat Ikhwan as-Safa al-Ijtima'iyah wa al-Akhlaqiyah* (Baghdad: Ma'arif Press, 1958), pp. 69-70.

30. See H. Spencer, *The Principles of Sociology* (New York: D. Appleton, 1895), pp. 426-427; Barnes, "Herbert Spencer and the Evolutionary Defense of Individualism" p. 118; Durkheim, *The Division of Labor in Society*, pp. 96, 103, 104; Nisbet, *op. cit.*, p. 33.

31. IK-FR, I:291.

32. IK–FR, I:302–303.

33. IK–FR, II:329.

34. IK–FR, II:417; Rosenthal, *op. cit.*, pp. 317, 318; M. Alam, "Ibn Khaldun's Concept of the Origin, Growth and Decay of Cities," *Islamic Culture*, Vol. 23 (April 1960), p. 91; H. K. Sherwani, *Studies in Muslim Political Thought and Administration* (Lahore: Sh. Muhammad Ashraf, 1959), p. 196.

35. See Durkheim's *Elementary Forms of Religious Life*, p. 16; Timasheff, *op. cit.*, p. 162.

36. I. L. Horowitz, "Introduction," in L. Gumplowicz, *Outlines of Sociology* (New York: Paine-Whitman Publishers, 1963), p. 27. Some writers equate functionalism with Marxism. See. F. Baali and J. Price, "Ibn Khaldun and Karl Marx: On Economic and Social Interpretation of History," *Arab Journal for the Humanities*, Vol. 1 (Winter 1981), pp. 341–342.

37. IK–FR, II:158.

38. IK–FR, I:90, 380–381; IK–FR, II:285.

39. *Op. cit.*, Vol. 2, p. 706.

40. IK–FR, I:327.

41. IK–FR,, I:327–328.

42. IK–FR, II:318.

43. IK–FR, III:282.

44. IK–FR, I:313. See also Hussein, *op. cit.*, p. 108; M. A. al-Jabiri, *Al-asabiyah wa al-Dawla* (Casablanca: Dar al-Thakafa, n.d.), pp. 248–249.

45. IK–FR, I:289.

46. See, for example, A. Hourani, *Arabic Thought in the Liberal Age: 1798–1939* (London: Oxford University Press, 1962), p. 78; Rabi' points out that T. Khemiri in his article "Der Asabiyah-Begriff in der *Muqaddima* des Ibn Haldun," *der Islam*, Vol. 22, 1936, pp. 184–185, "went to the extreme of equating *asabiyah* with Nationalität and argued that Ibn Khaldun's conception of *asabiyah* confirms with that of nationalism." See M. M. Rabi', *The Political Theory of Ibn Khaldun* (Leiden: Brill, 1967), p. 7. See also H. Ritter, "Irrational Solidarity Groups: A Socio-Psychological Study in Connection with Ibn

Khaldun," *Oriens,* Vol. 1 (1948), p. 22; and B. Spuler, "Ibn Khaldun the Historian," *A'mal Mahrajan Ibn Khaldun* (Cairo, 1962), p. 253.

47. See E. B. Tylor, *Primitive Culture* (London: J. Murray, 1871).

48. IK–FR, II:411, 416: IK–FR, III:137.

49. IK–FR, II:417.

50. IK–FR, III:282.

51. IK–FR, II:418.

52. IK–FR, II:419, 421.

53. IK–FR, II:419, also 418, 424.

54. IK–FR, II:117–118. See also IK–FR, III:359.

55. IK–FR, I:56, 57.

56. IK–FR, I:58, 299.

57. See P. A. Sorokin, *Contemporary Sociological Theory* (New York: Harper, 1928), p. 10; P. A. Sorokin, *Society, Culture, and Personality* (New York: Cooper Square Publishers, 1962), p. 23; H. Z. Ülken, "Ibn Khaldoun, Initiateur de la sociologie," *A'mal Mahrajan Ibn Khaldun* (Cairo: 1962), p. 40; A. W. Wafi, *Abd al-Rahman ibn Khaldun* (Cairo: Maktabat Misr, 1961), p. 212; H. K. Sherwani, *Studies in Muslim Political Thought and Administration* (Lahore: Sh. Muhammad Ashraf, 1959), p. 215.

58. Becker and Barnes, *op. cit.,* Vol. 1, p. 278, 350–351, 354; G. E. Cairns, *Philosophies of History* (New York: Citadel Press, 1962), pp. 322–323. See Sorokin, *Society, Culture, and Personality,* p. 23; Sorokin, *Contemporary Sociological Theory,* p. 100.

59. IK–FR, I:169.

60. IK–FR, I:170, 173, 174.

61. IK–FR, I:171.

62. IK–FR, I:174.

63. IK–FR, I:175–176.

64. IK–FR, I:176.

65. IK–FR, II:416–419.

66. IK–FR, II:433, 434; IK–FR, III:300.

67. IK-FR, II:421.

68. IK-FR, II:421-422; 425.

69. IK-FR, III:180, 181.

70. IK-FR, I:371.

71. IK-FR, III:307. See also IK-FR, II:431-435.

72. IK-FR, III:388. See also IK-FR, III:37, 289.

73. IK-FR, II:254, 354.

74. IK-FR, II:425.

75. *Ibid.*

76. IK-FR, III:249.

77. IK-FR, I:299. See also IK-FR, I:279, 300. Hence the incorrect statement by T. Hussein that Ibn Khaldun did not do more than to explain in some detail the saying "the common people follow the religion of the ruler." Hussein, *op. cit.*, p. 50. Ibn Khaldun said: "The ruler's subjects imitate him, because they see perfection in him, exactly as children imitate their parents, or students their teachers" (IK-FR, I:300). Hussein, however, was correct in classifying Ibn Khaldun's other types of imitation: (1) the victor imitates the vanquished; and (2) the vanquished imitates the victor. "The vanquished can always be observed to assimilate themselves to the victor in the use and style of dress" and in many other ways (IK-FR, I:299). Some of Ibn Khaldun's brief ideas on imitation are similar to those of Tarde. This is specifically true of the second type mentioned above. Tarde believed that "imitation proceeds from the socially superior to the socially inferior." See S. E. Grupp, "The Sociology of Gabriel Tarde (1843-1904)," *Sociology and Social Research*, Vol. 52 (July 1968), p. 343.

78. IK-FR, I:263.

79. *Ibid.*

80. IK-FR, I:264.

81. IK-FR, I:254.

82. E. Rosenthal *op. cit.*, p. 320.

83. IK-FR, II:419, 426.

84. IK-FR, III:292.

85. IK-FR, III:293–294. Ibn Khaldun emphasized that not all people study sciences. "The study of science is a luxury or convenience." IK-FR, I:85. See also IK-FR, III:290, 291, 295.

86. IK-FR, II:430, IK-FR, III:106.

87. See IK-FR, II:418–419. The goal of education, according to Ibn Khaldun, is knowledge in its many ramifications, not only to prepare leaders and governors.

88. IK-FR, III:360. Emphasis added. Ibn Khaldun asserted that a person whose language is not Arabic finds it more difficult than the Arabic speaking people to learn it. IK-FR, III:315, 383, 392.

89. IK-FR, I:79.

90. IK-FR, III:281–283.

91. IK-FR, III:316. "The same relationship of ideas with words and writing exists in every language." *Ibid.*

92. IK-FR, III:317, 318.

93. IK-FR, I:254.

94. IK-FR, II:48–49, 395.

95. See *Ras'il Ikhwan al-Safa*, Vol. 1, pp. 132–133; Vol. 2, pp. 134, 179; Vol. 4, pp. 146–147. The influence of music on human emotion was also mentioned by Aristotle. See F. Baali, "Ikhwan al-Safa and the Music," *Al-Adeeb* (October 1953); F. Baali, *Falsafat Ikhwan as-Safa, op. cit.*, pp. 104–109.

96. IK-FR, I:258. See also IK-FR, II:318.

97. Comte, *op. cit.*; H. E. Barnes, "The Social Political Philosophy of Auguste Comte: Positivist Utopia and the Religion of Humanity," pp. 105–106.

98. Durkheim, *The Division of Labor in Society*, p. 423.

99. Charles H. Cooley, *Human Nature and the Social Order* (New York: Charles Scribner's Sons, 1962), p. 152.

100. G. H. Mead, *Mind, Self and Society* (Chicago: University of Chicago Press, 1934), pp. 152–164.

101. C. Wright Mills, "Language, Logic, and Culture," *American Sociological Review*, Vol. 4 (October 1939), p. 673.

102. "Prophets in their religious propaganda depended on groups and families, they were the ones who could have been supported by God with anything in existence, if He had wished, but in His Wisdom He permitted matters to take their customary course" (IK–FR, I:324).

103. IK–FR, I:92–93.

104. IK–FR, I:261.

105. IK–FR, I:291.

106. IK–FR, I:84, 92, 262, 389–390.

107. IK–FR, I:448.

108. IK–FR, I:305.

109. See Comte, op. cit., p. 528; Durkheim, *Elementary Forms of Religious Life*, pp. 474–475; E. Durkheim, *Selected Writings*, ed. and trans. by A. Giddens (Cambridge: Cambridge University Press, 1972), pp. 228–233, 243–245; M. Weber, *From Max Weber* (New York: Oxford University Press, 1946), pp. 273–274, 283, 286–290; Tönnies, op. cit., pp. 63–64, 189, 219–226, 247.

110. IK–FR, I:386.

111. IK–FR, I:79–80; IK–FR, II:106. Ibn Khaldun discussed in some detail the functions of the judge and the police. See IK–FR, I:452–461.

112. IK–FR, II:108.

113. IK–FR, II:106–107. In relation to this statement, Durkheim maintained that if rules are not followed and respected, human society can no longer influence the individual. Durkheim, *The Division of Labor in Society*, p. 109 and *passim*.

114. IK–FR, I:307. Ibn Khaldun is against beating the young. Severe punishment specifically does harm to them. "It makes them feel oppressed and causes them to lose their energy. It makes them lazy and induces them to lie and be insincere. . . . They lose the quality that goes with social and political organization and makes people human . . . ." IK–FR, III:305. See also IK–FR, I:259, 261, 463.

115. IK–FR, II:107–108. See also IK–FR, I:366, 368, 385–386; IK–FR, II:93–100, 103–106, 109–111, 118–124, 283–286. Ibn Khaldun anticipated some of our time's events. The impact of the corruption of the rulers and their entourage on political and economic life is discussed in Chapters 5 and 6.

Chapter 4

1. See H. Simon, *Ibn Khalduns Wissenschaft von der Menschlichen Kultur* (Leipzig, 1959), p. 57; F. Rosenthal, "Introduction" to Ibn Khaldun, *The Muqaddimah: An Introduction to History* (Princeton: Princeton University Press, 1967), pp. lxxviii–lxxix.

2. Simon, *Ibid.*, pp. 51–52.

3. See A. Schimmel, *Ibn Chaldun, Ausgewahlte Abschnitte aus der muqaddima* (Tubingen, 1951).

4. See E. Will's review of G. Nebels' *Sokrates* in *Revue Historique* (October–December 1970), p. 445.

5. IK–FR, I:277.

6. IK–FR, I:284–285.

7. IK–FR, I:289; IK–FR, II:87.

8. P. K. Hitti, *History of the Arabs*, 3rd ed. (London: Macmillan, 1946), p. 27.

9. É. Durkheim, *The Division of Labor in Society*, trans. by G. Simpson (New York: The Free Press, 1933), p. 133.

10. *Ibid.*, p. 129.

11. *Ibid.*, p. 106; É. Durkheim, *Elementary Forms of Religious Life*, trans. by J. W. Swain (London: George Allen and Unwin, 1971), p. 16.

12. Durkheim, *The Division of Labor in Society*, p. 96.

13. *Ibid.*, p. 84.

14. *Ibid.*, pp. 104–105.

15. *Ibid.*, pp. 90–91, 102, 103.

16. H. Ritter, "Irrational Solidarity Groups: A Socio-Psychological Study in Connection with Ibn Khaldun," *Oriens*, Vol. 1 (1948), p. 2; M. A. Enan, *Ibn Khaldun: His Life and Work* (Lahore: Sh. Muahmmad Ashraf, 1969), pp. 168–171.

17. G. Vico, *The New Science*, (Ithaca, N. Y.: Cornell University Press, 1968). See also Simmel's analysis of group self-preservation. G. Simmel. *On Individuality and Social Forms*, ed. by D. N. Levine (Chicago: University of Chicago Press, 1971), pp. 7–8 *et seq.*; G. Simmel, *Conflict and the Web of Group-Affiliations* (Glencoe, Ill.: The Free Press, 1955), pp. 17–18; R. Heberle, "The Sociology of Georg Simmel:

The Forms of Social Interaction," in H. E. Barnes (ed.), *An Introduction to the History of Sociology* (Chicago: University of Chicago Press, 1949), p. 259.

18. *E. g.*, A. J. Toynbee, *A Study of History* (New York: Oxford University Press, 1962), Vol. 3, pp. 473-474; M. A. M. Nour, "Ibn Khaldun Ka-Mufakir Ijtima'i Arabi," *A'mal Mahrajan Ibn Khaldun* (Cairo, 1962), pp. 84-119; E. Gellner, *Muslim Society* (Cambridge: Cambridge University Press, 1981), pp. 17-20, 24-38, 72-95, 174-175, 180, 224.

19. See F. Baali and A. Wardi, *Ibn Khaldun and Islamic Thought-Styles: A Social Perspective* (Boston: G. K. Hall, 1981), p. 127. This interpretation is different from that of Z. al-Khadairi, *Falsafat al-Tarikh ind Ibn Khaldun* (Cairo: Dar al-Thakafa, 1979); A. Shrait, *Al-Fikr al-Akhlaki ind Ibn Khaldun* (Tunis: National Publishing Co., 1975); M. A. Lahbabi, *Ibn Khaldun: Presentation, Choix de texts, bibliographie* (Paris: Seghers, 1968).

20. Ritter, *op. cit.*, pp. 19-20. According to Ritter, "blood relationship is the strongest bond, especially for Semitic nations, at any rate for the Arabs." *Ibid.*, p. 20. See also al-Husri, *Dirasat an Muqaddimat Ibn Khaldun* (Beirut: Dar al-Kashshaf, 1943), p. 320; al-Khadairi, *op. cit.*, p. 180.

21. See for example IK-FR, I:295; Ritter, *op. cit.*, pp. 19, 40; Will, *loc. cit.*,; B. Spuler, "Ibn Khaldun the Historican," *A'mal Mahrajan Ibn Khaldun* (Cairo, 1962), p. 353.

22. Including backwoods villages. See G. Bouthout, *Ibn Khaldoun: sa philosophie sociale* (Paris, 1930), pp. 43-44, 52-62; P. A. Sorokin, *et al.*, *A Systematic Source Book in Rural Sociology* (Minneapolis: University of Minnesota Press, 1930), Vol. 1, pp. 58-59, 65-68.

23. Rabi', *op. cit.*, p. 54; J. J. Spengler, "Economic Thought of Islam: Ibn Khaldun," *Comparative Studies in Society and History*, Vol. 6 (1963-1964), pp. 290, 292, 294-295; G. Sarton, *Introduction to the History of Science* (Baltimore, Md.; Williams and Wilkins, 1948), Vol. 3, p. 1171; H. Z. Ülken, "Ibn Khaldoun: Initiateur de la sociologie," *A'mal Mahrajan Ibn Khaldun* (Cairo, 1962), p. 29; H. K. Sherwani, *Studies in Muslim Political Thought and Administration* (Lahore: Sh. Muhammad Ashraf, 1959), pp. 187-188, 196.

24. See, for example, Durkheim, *The Division of Labor in Society*, pp. 399, 341; S. Lukes, *Émile Durkheim — His Life and Work* (New York: Penguin Books, 1973), pp. 463-467, 471.

25. Vico, *op. cit.*, p. 426.

26. IK-FR, I:93. The *asabiyah* did not prevent the Arabs from relying on non-Arab and non-Muslim elements of the population, especially in science, arts, and literature.

27. IK-FR, I:324-327, 419.

28. IK-FR, II:301.

29. IK-FR, I:269, 270, 360.

30. IK-FR, I:292-293; 380-381.

31. IK-FR, I:331.

32. IK-FR, 1:351.

33. IK-FR, I:309-310.

34. Husri, *op. cit.*, p. 285; Baali and Wardi, *op. cit.*, pp. 108, 110, and *passim*.

35. It can be said here that *asabiyah* in the nomadic culture can be paralleled with a political party in civilization. It is for the welfare of people to have a caliph or a ruler from the strongest party in the nation. Abd al-Rahman Ibn Khaldun, *Al-Muqaddimah* (Beirut: Dar al-Kashshaf, n.d.), pp. 193-196, 216-224.

36. Abu Dhar al-Ghifari.

37. *Koran*, ch. 110, verse 3. Immediately after the death of Muhammad, the Arab tribes abandoned Islam in the same way they entered it, "in shoals." Nicholson pointed out that although the Arabs "became Moslems en masse, the majority of them neither believed in Islam nor knew what it meant." R. A. Nicholson, *A Literary History of the Arabs* (Cambridge: Cambridge University Press, 1930), p. 178. Generally, Nicholson's conclusion can be called right only in relation to the tribal spirit. The Arabs seemed to be unable to replace the age-old narrow spirit of the tribe with the wider spirit of Islam. In spite of the Prophet's persistent condemnation of the tribal spirit, the Arabs continued to be, consciously or unconsciously, influenced by it. This may be attributed to the fact that some cultural traditions and mores may not be easily overcome by new systems of belief and worship.

38. Hitti, *op. cit.*, p. 119.

39. *Ibn Khaldun, op. cit.*, p. 159-161.

40. *Ibid.*, especially p. 196, also p. 189.

41. IK–FR, 1:287–289.

42. Abd al-Rahman Ibn Khaldun, *Al Muqaddimah* (Beirut: Dar Ihia'a al-Turath al-Arabi, n.d.), p. 141.

43. IK–FR, I:334, also 270, 305, 307–308, 318.

44. IK–FR, I:334.

45. See Gellner, *op. cit.*, p. 224.

46. *Ibid.*, p. 57.

47. *Arab Times* (Kuwait, June 30, 1984), p. 1.

Chapter 5

1. IK–FR, I:284, 286, 288–289, 414; IK–FR, II:120, 301.

2. IK–FR, I:286.

3. *Ibid.*, also 328.

4. IK–FR, I:285.

5. IK–FR, I:80, 84, 92, 291, 380, 381, 385, 386, 389–390, 414, 473; IK–FR, II:137.

6. IK–FR, I:383.

7. IK–FR, I:395.

8. IK–FR, I:390.

9. IK–FR, I:305, 306, IK–FR, II:135.

10. IK–FR, I:473.

11. IK–FR, I:280, 292.

12. IK–FR, I:280.

13. IK–FR, I:383.

14. IK–FR, I:384.

15. IK–FR, I:385.

16. IK–FR, I:386.

17. IK–FR, II:3–4, 23.

18. IK-FR, III:308-309.

19. IK-FR, III:309, 310.

20. IK-FR, III:310.

21. IK-FR, I:295.

22. IK-FR, I:332.

23. IK-FR, II:94, 95, 96, 109-111, 316, 325.

24. IK-FR, II:96.

25. IK-FR, II:99.

26. IK-FR, II:328.

27. IK-FR, II:108-109, also 106-107.

28. IK-FR, II:106.

29. IK-FR, II:110.

30. IK-FR, I:386-387.

31. See H. Kohn, "Messianism," *Encyclopedia of Social Sciences*, 1931, Vol. 10, p. 363; D. S. Margoliouth, "Mahdi," *Encyclopedia of Religion and Ethics*, 1908, Vol. 8, pp. 336-340; D. M. Donaldson, *Aqidat al-Shi'ah* (Cairo: Sa'ada Press, 1933), pp. 230-231.

32. This seems to be the most acceptable interpretation of the term Mahdi. See Margoliouth, *op. cit.*, p. 336; and P. K. Hitti, *Makers of Arab History* (New York: Harper, 1968), p. 96.

33. IK-FR, I:298; IK-FR, II:118-119.

34. IK-FR, I:305-308, 320-321, 322.

35. IK-FR, I:386-387.

36. IK-FR, I:296, 351-352.

37. IK-FR, II:318.

38. IK-FR, I:286-287, 352, 378.

39. IK-FR, I:372.

40. IK-FR, I:377-378.

41. IK-FR, II:119.

42. IK-FR, II:306. Ibn Khaldun's ideas here resemble Toynbee's thought concerning the dominant minority. See Chapter 6.

43. IK-FR, II:337, also 332.

44. *Ibid.*

45. *Ibid.*, also I:383, 385.

46. IK-FR, II:99.

47. IK-FR, I:304.

48. IK-FR, II:98-99, also 123-124.

49. IK-FR, II:93.

50. *Ibid.* See also IK-FR, I:366-368.

51. IK-FR, II:117.

52. IK-FR, II:305.

53. IK-FR, I:328-329, also 331-332.

54. IK-FR, II:129. See also IK-FR, I:468-470.

55. IK-FR, I:287, 300-301.

56. See IK-FR, I:61-62, 275, 288.

57. See H. G. Wells, *Outline of History* (New York: Garden City Publishing Co., 1932), pp. 215-216.

58. See F. Baali, *Falsafat Ikhwan al-Safa al-Ijtima'iyah wa al-Akhlaqiyah* (Baghdad: Ma'arif Press, 1958), pp. 76-78, 86-93; F. Baali, "Madinat Ikhwan al-Safa al-Fadilah," *al-Aklam* (Baghdad, October 1966), pp. 101-105.

59. IK-FR, II:138.

60. See M. A. Enan, *Ibn Khaldun: His Life and Work* (Lahore: Sh. Muhammad Ashraf, 1969), p. 177.

61. N. Machiavelli, *The Prince*, trans. by L. Ricci (New York: The New American Library, 1952), p. 66, also p. 65.

62. *Ibid.*, p. 72, also p. 73.

63. H. Ritter, "Irrational Solidarity Groups: A Socio-Psychological Study in Connection with Ibn Khaldun," *Orien*, Vol. 1 (1948), pp. 2, 40.

64. See W. G. Sumner and A. G. Keller, *Science of Society* (New Haven, Conn.: Yale University Press, 1927). pp. 704, 709. See also W. Durant, *The Story of Civilization* (New York: Simon and Schuster, 1942), p. 23.

65. H. Becker and H. E. Barnes, *Social Thought from Lore to Science* (New York: Dover Publications, 1961), Vol. 1, pp. 349–351, 357–358; Vol. 2, pp. 707–708.

66. Charles de Secondat Montesquieu, *The Spirit of the Laws*, trans. by T. Nugent (New York: Hafner, 1949), p. 25.

67. *Ibid.*, p. 27.

68. *Ibid.*, p. 115.

69. *Ibid.*, p. 116.

70. *Ibid.*

71. See R. Heberle, "The Sociology of Georg Simmel: The Forms of Social Interaction," in H. E. Barnes (ed.), *An Introduction to the History of Sociology* (Chicago: University of Chicago Press, 1948), p. 259.

72. A. Comte, *Positive Philosophy* (New York: Calvin Blanchard, 1855), pp. 498, 508, and *passim*. See also N. S. Timasheff, *Sociological Theory: Its Nature and Growth* (New York: Random House, 1967), pp. 23–24; H. E. Barnes, "The Social Political Philosophy of Auguste Comte: Positivist Utopia and the Religion of Humanity," in Barnes (ed.), *op. cit.*, pp. 88–89, 96; Becker and Barnes, *op. cit.*, Vol. 2, pp. 573, 575, 576, 710.

73. F. Oppenheimer, *The State* (New York: Vanguard Press, 1922), pp. 27, 279.

74. *Ibid.*, p. 27. See also pp. 3, 31, 45, 54, 56 *et seq.*

75. M. Weber, *From Max Weber: Essays in Sociology*, trans. by H. H. Gerth and C. Wright Mills (New York: Oxford University Press, 1946), pp. 173, 178.

76. M. Weber, *The Theory of Social and Economic Organization* (New York: The Free Press, 1947), pp. 341, 342.

Chapter 6

1. Abd al-Rahman Ibn Khaldun, *Al-Muqaddimah* (Beirut: Dar Ahia' al-Turath al-Arabi, n.d.), pp. 175–176. The process of the state formation and decline is "like the silkworm that spins and then, in turn, finds its end amidst the threads itself has spun" (IK–FR, I:297).

2. See M. M. Rabi', *The Political Theory of Ibn Khaldun* (Leiden: E. J. Brill, 1967), pp. 42, 54–55; M. Madhi, *Ibn Khaldun's Philosophy: A Study in the Philosophic Foundation of the Science of Culture* (Chicago: University of Chicago Press, 1964), p. 268.

3. See F. Baali and A. Wardi, *Ibn Khaldun and Islamic Thought-Styles: A Social Perspective* (Boston: G. K. Hall, 1981), p. 137.

4. H. Simon, *Ibn Khalduns Wissenschaft von der Menschlichen Kultur* (Leipzig, 1959), p. 69.

5. IK–FR, I:280–281.

6. IK–FR, II:268.

7. Or Sufi, an Islamic mystical cult.

8. The following statement by Engels is remarkably similar to Ibn Kahldun's social dialectic:

Islam is a religion that is adapted for Orientals, especially Arabs, that is, for urbanites employed in commerce and trade on one hand, and for nomadic Bedouins on the other. But herein lies the germ of periodically recurring collision. The urbanites become rich, luxuriant, and lax in the observance of the 'Law'. The Bedouins – poor, and austere because of their poverty – look forward enviously and greedily upon these riches and pleasures. Then they unite under a prophet, the Mahdi, in order to punish the apostates, to reestablish respect for the ceremonial law and the true faith, and to pocket the treasures of the renegades as a reward. Of course, after a hundred years they are in the same position as the former apostates; a new purification of religion is necessary, a new Mahdi stands up, the game begins anew. These are all movements camouflaged with religion, they have economic causes; but, even when they are victorious, they let the old economic conditions go on. Thus everything remains the same, and the collision becomes periodical (*The New Times*, I[1894–95], p.5). (German.)

Whether Engels knew Ibn Khaldun's work this is a question which can be raised. Although no definite evidence can be found, Simon states that the French translation of Ibn Khaldun's work, in the 1860s, could very well have reached Engels and Marx who were very much interested in new objective and systematic publications. See Simon, *op. cit.*, p. 65.

9. Simon, *ibid.*, p. 121, also p. 74. See. O. G. von Wesendonk, "Ibn Chaldun, ein arabischer Kulturhistoriker des 14. Jahrhunderts," *Deutsche Rundschau*, Vol. 49 (1923); M. A. Enan, *Ibn Khaldun: His Life and Work* (Lahore: Sh. Muhammd Ashraf, 1969), pp. 161–162.

10. See N. Schmidt, *Ibn Khaldun: Historian, Sociologist and Philosopher* (New York: Columbia University Press, 1930), p. 21.

11. See, for example, R. Chambliss, *Social Thought from Hammurabi to Comte* (New York: Dryden, 1954), pp. 308, 311; H. Z. Ülken, "Ibn Khaldoun Initiateur de la sociologie," *A'mal Mahrajan Ibn Khaldun* (Cairo, 1962) , p. 37; M. A. M. Nour, "An Analytical Study of the Sociological Thought of Ibn Khaldun, "dissertation (Lexington: University of Kentucky, 1953), p. 184; and T. Hussein, *Étude analytique et critique de la philosophie sociale d' Ibn Khaldoun* (Paris: A. Pedone, 1917), p. 102.

12. B. C. Busch, "Divine Intervention in *The Muqaddimah* of Ibn Khaldun," *History of Religion.* Vol. 7 (May 1968), p. 328.

13. See Simon, *op. cit.*, pp. 74, 75.

14. See J. Spengler, "Economic Thought of Islam: Ibn Khaldun," *Comparative Studies in Society and History*, Vol. 6 (1963–1964), p. 272; Chambliss, *op. cit.*, p. 415.

15. See M. A. Lahbabi, *Ibn Khaldoun: Presentation, Choix de texts, bibliographie* (Paris: Seghers, 1968), pp. 39, 41.

16. See, for example, H. Becker and H. E. Barnes, *Social Thought from Lore to Science* (New York: Dover Publications, 1961), Vol. 2, pp. 706–708.

17. *Ibid.*, Vol. 2, p. 741.

18. *Ibid.*, See also H. E. Barnes, "The Social Philosophy of Ludwig Gumplowicz – The Struggle of Races and Social Groups," in H. E. Barnes (ed.), *An Introduction to the History of Sociology* (Chicago: University of Chicago Press, 1948), p. 203.

19. See Becker and Barnes, *op. cit.*, Vol. 1, p. 267. These two writers call Oppenheimer a "reviver of the theories of Ibn Khaldun," *ibid.*, Vol 2, p. 721.

20. *Ibid.*, p. 278.

21. See Y. Locoste, *Ibn Khaldoun: naissance de l'historie passe du tiers monde*, trans. by M. Sulaiman. (Beirut: Ibn Khaldun House, 1973), p. 155.

22. See A. J. Toynbee, *A Study of History* (New York: Oxford University Press, 1962), Vol. 3, p. 291; Becker and Barnes, *op. cit.*, Vol. 1, p. 200; Simon, *op. cit.*, p. 29.

23. G. E. Cairns, *Philosophies of History* (New York: Citadel Press, 1962), pp. 255, 276.

24. Spengler, *op. cit.*, p. 283.

25. G. Vico, *The New Science*, trans. by T. G. Bergin and M. H. Fisch (Ithaca, N. Y.: Cornell University Press, 1968), p. 104, (para. 349). Excerpts are used by permission of the Publisher.

26. *Ibid.*, pp. 78-79 (para. 241-242); pp. 338-339.

27. *Ibid.*, p. 423 (para. 1105); IK-FR, II:293-294.

28. Cairns, *op. cit.* p. 347.

29. Vico, *op. cit.*

30. IK-FR, II:329. Ibn Khaldun bitterly attacked those men of knowledge who look down on the men of power and belittle the significance of their social role. He considered this superciliousness unjustified and rude. He seemed to prefer those yes-men who try to propitiate, please, and flatter any power holder, and consequently obtain wealth and position. See IK-FR, II:329-334.

31. A. R. J. Turgot, *A Philosophical Review*, trans. by Ronald L. Meek (Cambridge: University Press, 1973), p. 75. Excerpt is reprinted with the permission of the publisher. See also Becker and Barnes, *op. cit.*, Vol. 1, pp. 413-414.

32. See Cairns, *op. cit.*, p. 292. Venable believes that Marx and Engels always "speak of classless socialism as the next stage, not the final stage of history, and everywhere they imply and frequently explicitly assert the impossibility of any social or historical finality." V. Venable, *Human Nature: The Marxian View* (New York: Alfred A. Knopf, 1945), p. 174.

It is interesting to note, according to Cairns (*op. cit.*, p. 295), that "The picture of the state of man when the cycle of the dialectic is fulfilled resembles the Kingdom of Heaven idea of Christianity. It is man's return to Eden (primitive communism for the Marxist) but at a much higher developmental level."

33. K. Marx and F. Engels, *The Communist Manifesto* (New York: International Publishers, 1964), p. 57.

34. Israel points out that dialectical materialism is concerned with problems of epistemology; historical materialism with sociological-economic problems seen in a historical perpective. J. Israel, *Alienation: From Marx to Modern Sociology* (Boston: Allyn and Bacon, 1971), p. 91. See also G. K. Zollschan and W. Hirsch (eds.), *Social Change: Explorations, Diagnoses, and Conjectures* (New York: Wiley, 1976), p. 168.

35. K. Marx and F. Engels, *The German Ideology* (New York: International publishers, 1947), p. 7; F. Baali and J. B. Price, "Ibn Khaldun and Karl Marx: On Economic and Social Interpretation of History," *Arab Journal for the Humanities*, Vol. 1 (Winter 1981), p. 339.

36. I. L. Horowitz, "Introduction," in L. Gumplowicz, *Outline of Sociology* (New York: Paine-Whitman Publishers, 1963), p. 36. See also H. E. Barnes, "The Social Psychology of Ludwig Gumplowicz," *op. cit.*, p. 193.

37. Barnes, *ibid.*, p. 197, also pp. 198–201.

38. G. Sarton, *Introduction to the History of Science* (Baltimore, Md.: Williams and Wilkins, 1948), Vol. 3, p. 1770. See also Cairns, *op. cit.*, p. 322.

39. O. Spengler, *The Decline of the West*, trans. by Charles Atkinson (New York: Alfred A. Knopf, 1932); P. A. Sorokin, *Sociological Theories of Today* (New York: Harper and Row, 1966), p. 188; H. Becker *et al.*, *Contemporary Social Theory* (New York: Appleton-Century, 1940), pp. 533–535.

40. See Sorokin, *ibid.*, p. 189.

41. *Ibid.*

42. P. A. Sorokin, *The Crisis of Our Age* (New York: E. P. Dutton, 1946), p. 19.

43. Cairns, *op. cit.*, pp. 380–381, also pp. 382–401.

44. *Ibid.*, pp. 388–389; Sorokin, *Crisis of Our Age*, p. 103.

45. See Sorokin's explanation in his *Sociological Theory of Today*, pp. 613–649.

46. See H. Becker and A. Boskoff (eds.) *Modern Sociological Theory* (New York: Dryden Press, 1957), p. 283.

47. IK-FR, I:278.

48. IK–FR, I:301.

49. IK–FR, I:386.

50. R. F. Butts, "Arnold J. Toynbee's Philosophy of History," *Educational Theory*, Vol. 22 (Winter 1972), p. 4.

51. *Ibid.*, p. 5. See also Cairns, *op. cit.*, pp. 279, 455; H. E. Barnes, "Arnold Toynbee: Orosius and Augustine in Modern Dress," in Barnes (ed.), *op. cit.*, p. 723.

52. Toynbee, *op. cit.*, p. 187.

53. Butts, *op. cit.*, pp. 8, 9. Ibn Khaldun himself provided an interesting example of Toynbee's process of "withdrawal-and-return." By withdrawing to a peaceful refuge among Awlad Arif and freeing himself from the turmoils and disturbances of civilization, Ibn Khaldun was able to contemplate deeply in order to discover a solution for his own overwhelming dilemma. He was, in other words, ready to receive the intuitive insight, or what Bergson calls the mystical inspiration of the *élan vital*. When Ibn Khaldun returned from his historic withdrawal, and became, to use Toynbee's terminology, a "transfigured personality," he was perhaps expecting that such a benevolent system was about to rise. The rulers whom he served before his withdrawal began to appear, to his eyes, unworthy of his service. He probably began to consider them representative of the phase of decline in the social dialectic.

54. *Ibid.*, pp. 11–13, pp. 17–18. See also Cairns, *op. cit.*, p. 430; D. Martindale, *The Nature and Types of Sociological Theory* (Boston: Houghton Mifflin, 1960), pp. 113–115.

55. Cairns, *op. cit.*, p. 420.

56. See ibid, p. 421. A brief passage in Montesquieu's *Considerations on the Causes of the Grandeur and Decadence of the Romans* seems to approach the cyclical pattern: "There are general causes, whether moral or physical . . . which operate in every monarchy to bring about its rise, its duration, and its fall." See the French text, Montesquieu's *Considerations sur les causes de la grandeur de Romains*, p. 103; R. Aron, *Main Currents in Sociological Thought* (New York: Anchor Books, 1968), Vol. 1, pp. 14–15.

57. Cairns, *op. cit.*, p. 353.

58. Cairns, *op. cit.*, p. 336.

59. *Ibid.*, p. 462; also pp. 323–324, 343, 349, 352, 421.

60. According to Speier, "Sorokin's basic distinction between *sensate, idealistic,* and *ideational* bears more than a faint resemblance to the ideas expressed" by St. Augustine. H. Speier, "The Sociological Ideas of Pitirim Alexandrovitch Sorokin: 'Integralist' Sociology," in Barnes (ed.), *op. cit.,* p. 894. See also Cairns, *op. cit.,* pp. 278–279, 453; Becker and Boskoff, *op. cit.,* pp. 283–284.

61. Toynbee, *op. cit.,* p. 516.

62. See Simon, *op. cit.,* p. 64; E. Gellner, *Muslim Society* (Cambridge: Cambridge University Press, 1981), pp. 31, 54.

63. See Cairns, *op. cit.,* pp. 457–476.

Chapter 7

1. See IK–FR, I:252; II:235, 237, 291.

2. M. Alam, "Ibn Khaldun's Concept of the Origin, Growth and Decay of Cities," *Islamic Culture,* Vol. 34 (April 1960), p.101.

3. IK–FR, II:243–244.

4. IK–FR, II:237–238, 243–248.

5. IK–FR, II:246, 247.

6. IK–FR, II:237–238, also 241, 270, 271.

7. IK–FR, II:239, also 241, 242.

8. IK–FR, II:267–269.

9. IK–FR, II:269–270.

10. IK–FR, I:235.

11. Ibn Khaldun cited al-Khatib who stated in his *History* "that in the time of al-Ma'mun, the number of public baths in Baghdad reached 65,000." IK–FR, II:236, also 278.

12. See M. Mahdi, *Ibn Khaldun's Philosophy of History* (Chicago: University of Chicago Press, 1964), p. 203; Nour, *loc. cit.;* S. G. Shiber, "Ibn Khaldun: An Early Town Planner," *Middle East Forum,* Vol. 38 (March 1962), p. 28; IK–FR, II:270–271.

13. IK–FR, II:270.

14. IK–FR, II:361–363, also IK–FR, I:462.

15. IK-FR, II:235-236.

16. IK-FR, II:135-137, also I:64.

17. L. Wirth, "Urbanism as a Way of Life," *American Journal of Sociology*, Vol. 41 (July 1938), pp. 1-23. For a thorough critique of Wirth's urban "theory" see F. Baali and J. S. Vandiver, *Urban Sociology* (New York: Appleton-Century-Crofts, 1970), ch. 5,

18. IK-FR, II:106, also 235-236.

19. IK-FR, II:301.

20. IK-FR, II:302. Thus, more division of labor and specialization are expected in largely populated areas. Comte and Durkheim, for example, associated the increase of population density with greater specialization in the division of labor. Nashat contends that Ibn Khaldun who believed that an increase in population is accompanied by an increase in the level of living preceded Marshall who said that "an increase of population is likely to continue to be accompanied by a more than proportionate increase of the means of satisfying human needs." See A. Nashat, "Ibn Khaldoun: Pioneer Economist," *L'Egypte Contemporaine* (Cairo, 1945), Vol. 35, p. 424.

21. Likewise, the declining population of the city "entails a decrease in the crafts." IK-FR, II:270.

22. IK-FR, II:272.

23. *Ibid.*

24. IK-FR, II:273, also 348-352, 433; IK-FR, I:351.

25. IK-FR, II:292, 348.

26. IK-FR, II:295.

27. IK-FR, II:274, also 275.

28. IK-FR, I:299-300, 338-339, 341, 388; IK-FR, II:296, 297.

29. IK-FR, II:293-294.

30. IK-FR, II:295-296.

31. IK-FR, II:432, also 354-355.

32. See, for example, IK-FR, I:285-289, 293, 341-342, 351-352, 462; IK-FR, II:299-300; E. I. J. Rosenthal, *Islam in the Modern National State* (Cambridge: Cambridge University Press, 1965), p. 20.

33. IK-FR, II:330.

34. IK-FR, II:427. See also IK-FR, III:300; C. Issawi, *An Arab Philosophy of History: Selections from the Prolegomena of Ibn Khaldun of Tunis, 1332-1406* (London: John Murray, 1950), p. 143.

35. IK-FR, III:4.

36. IK-FR, II:434.

37. IK-FR, II:406, also IK-FR, III:8, 31, 126, 148-149, 246.

38. Ikhwan al-Safa's ideas on the city are scattered here and there in their *Ras'il.* The present writer made the first effort to compile and organize their thoughts about their virtuous city. See F. Baali, *Falsaft Ikhwan al-Safa al-Ijtima'iyah wa al-Akhlaqiyah* (Baghdad: Ma'arif Press, 1958), ch. 3; F. Baali, "Medinat Ikhwan al-Safe al-Fadilah," *al-Aklam* (Baghdad, October 1966), pp. 101-105.

39. See. P. Wheatley, "The Concept of Urbanism," in P. J. Ucko *et al.* (eds.), *Man, Settlement and Urbanism* (London and Cambridge, Mass.: Schenkman Publishing Co., 1972), p. 601.

40. G. Vico, *The New Science,* trans. by T. G. Bergin and M. H. Fisch (Ithaca, N. Y.: Cornell University Press, 1968), p. 423 (para. 1105).

41. G. E. Cairns, *Philosophies of History* (New York: Citadel Press, 1962), p. 345. Bodin characterized the city inhabitants as "more subtle, politic, and cunning than those that lie far from the sea and from traffic." J. Bodin, *The Six Bookes of a Commonweale,* trans. by R. Knolles and ed. by K. D. McRae (Cambridge: Harvard University Press, 1962), pp. 564-568. Rousseau believed that luxury, pleasure, and leisure corrupt the character and make people lose the "good" qualities. G. Bouthoul, *Ibn Khaldoun: sa philosophie sociale* (Paris, 1930), p. 76.

42. Trans. by G. Simpson (New York: The Free Press, 1933), pp. 51-52. The excerpt is reprinted with permission of the publisher.

43. See D. Martindale, "Prefatory Remark," in M. Weber, *The City,* trans. and ed. by D. Martindale and G. Neuwirth (New York: The Free Press, 1958), pp. 18-19; J. Strong, *The Twentieth Century City* (New York: Baker and Taylor, 1898).

44. C. S. Fischer, "The Effect of Urban Life on Traditional Values," *Social Forces,* Vol. 53 (March 1975), pp. 421, 431. See also M. B. Clinard, "Deviant Behavior: Urban-Rural Contrast," in C. E. Elias, Jr.

et al. (eds.), *Metropolis: Values in Conflict* (Belmont, Calif.: Wadsworth, 1963); M. Argyle, "Religious Observance," in D. L. Sills (ed.), *International Encyclopedia of the Social Sciences* (New York: Macmillan Press, 1968); F. K. Willitis *et al.*, "Leveling of Attitudes in Mass Society," *Rural Sociology*, Vol. 38 (Spring 1973); M. E. Wolfgang, "Urban Crime," in J. Q. Wislon (ed.), *The Metropolitan Enigma* (New York: Anchor, 1970); I. Hoch, "Income and City Size," *Urban Studies*, Vol. 9 (October 1972).

45. IK-FR, II:106: Becker and Barnes, *op. cit.*, Vol. 1, pp. 274–275.

46. Cited by Wirth himself, *op. cit.*, p. 11.

47. G. Simmel, *The Sociology of Georg Simmel*, trans. by H. H. Gerth and C. Wright Mills, and ed. by K. H. Wolff (New York: The Free Press, 1950), pp. 413, also 408–410.

48. Durkheim, *op. cit.*, p. 339.

49. Wirth spoke of "the reserve, the indifference, and the blasé outlook which urbanites manifest in their relationships." Wirth, *op. cit.*, p. 12.

50. Simmel, *op. cit.*, pp. 412, 413, 414.

51. The city according to Spengler implies money power.

52. F. Oppenheimer, *The State* (New York: Vanguard Press, 1922), pp. 238, 241.

53. Wirth, *op. cit.*, pp. 16, 17–18.

54. IK-FR, II:287–288, 292.

55. See Martindale, *op. cit.*, pp. 12–16.

56. *E.g.*, W. Bascom, "Urbanization Among the Yoruba," *American Journal of Sociology*, Vol. 60 (March 1955), pp. 446–453.

57. See O. Lewis, "Urbanization Without Breakdown: A Case Study," *The Scientific Monthly*, Vol. 75 (July 1952). See Baali and Vandiver, *op. cit.*, pp. 119–120.

58. F. Baali, "Social Factors in Iraqi Rural-Urban Migration," *American Journal of Economics and Sociology*, Vol. 25 (October 1966), p. 364; F. Baali, *Relation of the People to the Land in Southern Iraq* (Gainesville: University of Florida Press, 1966), ch. 8; D. G. (Adams) Philips, *Iraq's People and Resources* (Berkely and Los Angeles: University of California Press, 1958); J. Abu-Lughod, "Migrant Adjustment to City Life: The Egyptian Case," *American Journal of Sociology*, Vol. 67

(July 1961), pp. 22-32; K. K. Petersen, "Villagers in Cairo: Hypotheses versus Data." *American Journal of Sociology*, Vol. 77 (November 1971), pp. 560-573.

59. Simon, *op. cit.*, p. 53.

60. See Wirth, *op. cit.*, p. 21.

61. IK-FR, II:303.

Chapter 8

1. IK-FR, I:250, 251, also 84-85; F. Baali's review of *Dirasat fi Tabi'at al-Mujtama' al 'Iraqi (A Study of Iraqi Society)* by Ali Wardi, *American Sociological Review*, Vol. 31 (December 1966), p. 883; A. al-Wardi, *Mantiq Ibn Khaldun* (Cairo: Institute of Arab Studies, 1962), pp. 86-90, 105.

2. IK-FR, I:249, also 250, 290; IK-FR, II:287, 316-317, 335-336, 356-357; IK-FR, III:151.

3. IK-FR, I:252-253.

4. *Ibid.*

5. IK-FR, II:106, 135-136, 235-236, 270, 272, 302, 361-362.

6. IK-FR, I:250-251; IK-FR, II:316, 357.

7. IK-FR, II:316-317, 335-336; IK-FR, III:151.

8. IK-FR, II:357, also, 317.

9. IK-FR, II:347, 348, also 266-267.

10. IK-FR, II:280.

11. IK-FR, I:177, 306.

12. IK-FR, I:84, 250.

13. IK-FR, I:177-182.

14. IK-FR, I:252, 257-258, 282, 287, 302; IK-FR, II:87, 248, 297.

15. IK-FR, II:280; F. Baali and A. Wardi, *Ibn Khaldun and Islamic Thought-Styles — A Social Perspective* (Boston: G. K. Hall, 1981), pp. 51-52.

16. IK-FR, I:261, also 298, 313.

17. IK-FR, I:241, 287, 314-319, 345; IK-FR, II:87, 291-297.

18. IK-FR, I:265-267, also 273-280.

19. IK-FR, I:253-254, 255.

20. IK-FR, II:293-294.

21. IK-FR, I:306, also 177-178; IK-FR, II:266-267.

22. IK-FR, I:179-180.

23. IK-FR, II:266.

24. IK-FR, 1:258-262.

25. IK-FR, I:258-260, 303-305.

26. IK-FR, III:4.

27. IK-FR, II:435.

28. IK-FR, III:149-150.

29. IK-FR, II:434.

30. IK-FR, II:427, also 346-348; IK-FR, III:126, 246.

31. IK-FR, II:432, 433, also, 406.

32. IK-FR, I:309.

33. IK-FR, I:309-310.

34. F. Benet, "The Ideology of Islamic Urbanization," *International Journal of Comparative Sociology,* Vol. 4 (September 1963), p. 214.

35. *Ibid.,* p. 215.

36. IK-FR, I:300-301.

37. IK-FR, I:304.

38. IK-FR, I:177-178, 289; IK-FR, II:293-294, 343-345, IK-FR, III:305-306.

39. IK-FR, II:330.

40. IK-FR, I:304. See also Baali and Wardi, *op. cit.,* pp. 108-109; E. I. J. Rosenthal, "Ibn Khaldun: A North African Muslim Thinker of the Fourteenth Century," *Bulletin of the John Rylands Library,* Vol. 24 (1940), p. 308; G. Bouthoul, *Ibn Khaldoun: sa philosophie sociale* (Paris, 1930), p. 6: H. Becker and H. E. Barnes, *Social Thought from Lore to Science (New York: Dover Publications, 1961), Vol. 1, p. 267; M. M. Rabi'*

The Political Theory of Ibn Khaldun (Leiden: E. J. Brill, 1967), p. 5; H. K. Sherwani, *Studies in Muslim Political Thought and Administration* (Lahore: Sh. Muhammad Ashraf, 1959), p. 195; H. Simon, *Ibn Khalduns Wissenschaft von der Menschlichen Kultur* (Leipzig, 1959), p. 107; H. Z. Ülken, "Ibn Khaldoun, Initiateur de la sociologie," *A'mal Madrahan Ibn Khaldun* (Cairo, 1962), p. 6; E. Will's review of G. Nebels's *Sokrates* in *Revue Historique* (October–December, 1970), p. 445.

41. IK–FR, III:314. Ibn Khaldun argued that his statement that "most of the scholars in Islam have been non-Arabs," should not be interpreted as a weakness in the original nature of the Arabs. Due to their simple conditions, the Arabs at the beginning of Islam had no sciences or crafts (IK–FR, III:311). Later, mainly because of their war efforts, the Arabs left "sciences" to Persians and others.

42. See H. Miner, "The Folk-Urban Continuum," *American Sociological Review*, Vol. 17 (October 1952), p. 534.

43. R. Heberle, "Ferdinand Tönnies' Contributions to the Sociology of Political Parties," *American Journal of Sociology*, Vol. 61 (May 1955), p. 213; R. Heberle, "Preface," in F. Tönnies, *Gemeinschaft and Gesellschaft*, (East Lansing: Michigan State University Press, 1957), p. x.

44. *Ibid.*, p. vii.

45. R. Heberle, "The Sociological System of Ferdinand Tonnies: 'Community' and 'Society,'" in H. E. Barnes (ed.) *An Introduction to the History of Sociology* (Chicago: University of Chicago Press, 1948), p. 243.

46. *Ibid.*

47. R. Chambliss, *Social Thought from Hammurabi to Comte* (New York: Dryden, 1954), p. 312.

48. Tönnies, *Gemeinschaft and Gesellschaft*, pp. 55–56; Heberle, "The Sociological System of Ferdinand Tönnies," pp. 240–241.

49. R. Heberle, "The Application of Fundamental Concepts in Rural Community Studies, *Rural Sociology*, Vol. 6 (September 1941), pp. 207, 208.

50. See *ibid.*, pp. 208–209; F. Baali, "Land Tenure and Rural Social Organization: A study in Southern Iraq," dissertation (Baton Rouge: Louisiana State University, 1960), pp. 17–19.

51. É. Durkheim, *The Division of Labor in Society*, trans. by G. Simpson (New York: The Free Press, 1933), pp. 79, 131; IK-FR, I:273-274, 284.

52. *Ibid.*, pp. 106, 133, 226; IK-FR, I:261, 265, and *passim*.

53. Durkheim, *ibid.*, p. 102, also 84, 90-91, 96, 102-104; J. D. McKinney, "Application of *Gemeinschaft* and *Gesellschaft* as related to Other Typologies," in Tönnies, *Gemeinschaft and Gesellschaft,op. cit.*, p. 13; IK-FR, I:257, 260-263, 284, 353.

54. Durkheim, *op. cit.*, pp. 126-127, 128; McKinney, *ibid*; IK-FR, I:259, also 257, 261, 262.

55. See Durkheim, *ibid.*, pp. 22, 23.

56. E. Gellner, *Muslim Society* (Cambridge: Cambridge University Press, 1981), pp. 87, also 39, 90.

57. See McKinney, *op. cit.*, p. 17.

58. P. A. Sorokin, *Sociological Theories of Today* (New York: Harper and Row, 1966), pp. 337, 341; H. Becker, "Sacred and Secular Societies Considered with Reference to Folk-State and Similar Classifications," *Social Forces*, Vol. 28 (May 1950), pp. 361-376.

Chapter 9

1. IK-FR, I:10, 11, 14, 71, 77-78.

2. É. Durkheim, *The Division of Labor in Society*, trans. by G. Simpson (New York: The Free Press, 1933), p. 399; IK-FR, I:79, 89-91, 291, 356, 358, 380, 389; IK-FR, II:137, 241, 302-303, 417.

3. G. E. Cairns, *Philosophies of History* (New York: The Citadel Press, 1962), p. 336. Ibn Khaldun is considered among the "outstanding early representatives" of conflict theory. See H. Becker and H. E. Barnes, *Social Thought from Lore to Science* (New York: Dover Publications, 1961), Vol. 2, p. 741.

4. IK-FR, I:106; IK-FR, II:106; L. Wirth, "Urbanism as a Way of Life," *American Journal of Sociology*, Vol. 41 (July 1938), pp. 1-24.

5. IK-FR, II:432.

6. P. A. Sorokin, "Forward," in F. Tönnies, *Gemeinschaft and Gesellschaft*, English trans. (East Lansing: Michigan State University Press, 1957), p. ix.

7. IK–FR, I:249.

8. Ibn Khaldun is regarded by several social scientists as the "earliest social exponent of the economic conception of history." R. Michels, *First Lectures in Political Sociology* (St. Paul: University of Minneapolis Press, 1949), p. 10.

9. Becker and Barnes, *op. cit.*, Vol. 1, p. 275.

10. According to Durkheim, "in the entire work of Spencer the problem of methodology occupies no place, for *The Study of Sociology*, perhaps a misleading title, is devoted to demonstrating the difficulties and possibilities of sociology, not to expounding the methods it ought to use." É. Durkheim, *The Rules of Sociological Method*, trans. by S. A. Solovay, and J. H. Mueller (New York: The Free Press, 1938), p. lix.

11. S. Lukes, *Émile Durkheim – His Life and Work: A Historical and Critical Study* (New York: Penguin Books, 1973), p. 479. See É. Durkheim, *The Elementary Forms of Religious Life* (Glencoe, Ill.: Free Press, 1974), p. 1.

12. J. D. Douglass and Associates, *Introduction to Sociology: Situations and Structures* (New York: The Free Press, 1973), p. 9

13. *The Sociological Imagination* (London: Oxford University Press, 1959), p. 47.

14. See, for example, N. J. Smelser, "Sociology and the Other Social Sciences," in P. F. Lazarsfeld *et al.* (ed.), *The Uses of Sociology* (New York: Basic Books, 1967); F. Adler, "The Basic Difficulty of Historical Sociology," *Sociological Quarterly*, Vol. 2 (January 1961); and W. J. Cahnman and A. Boskoff (eds.), *Sociology and History: Theory and Research* (New York: The Free Press, 1964).

15. See, for example, C. Brinton, *The Anatomy of Revolution* (Englewood Cliffs, N. J.: Prentice-Hall, 1952); and B. Moore, Jr., *Social Origins of Dictatorship and Democracy, Lord and Peasant in the Making of the Modern World.* (Boston: Beacon Press, 1966).

16. This is the definition used by Frederick Engles in *Anti-Duehring*, (New York: International Publishers, 1939), p. 29.

17. F. Baali, "Urbanization and Urbanism as a Mode of Life in the Gulf Region of the Southwest Asia," in progress.

18. A recent study of 341 randomly selected households in six residential areas of Kuwait City showed that despite urbanization and Westernization the family-kin ties are very strong. "Contact and

assistance in times of need is very extensive among *all* segments of the sample." F. Al-Thakeb, *Family-Kin Relationships in Contemporary Kuwait Society* (Kuwait: Annals of the Faculty of Arts, Kuwait University, 1982), Vol. 3, p. 70. (Emphasis added.)

19. IK–FR, I:286–287, 304, 352, 378, 386–387; IK–FR, II:94, 95, 96, 99, 332, 337.

20. "A science hardly born has not, nor could it have at the beginning, anything but a vague and uncertain sense of that sector of reality toward which it should be oriented." É. Durkheim, "The Realm of Sociology as a Science," trans. by E. K. Wilson, *Social Forces*, Vol. 59 (June 1981), p. 1054.

21. IK–FR, I:14. According to Durkheim: "Science is fragmentary and incomplete; it advances but slowly and is never finished." E. Durkheim, *The Elementary Forms of Religious Life*, p. 431.

22. IK–FR, III:481.

BIBLIOGRAPHY

Works in Arabic

Alim, Mahmud Amin al-. "Muqaddimat Ibn Khaldun," al-Fikr al-Arabi, 1 (November – December 1978).

Baali, Fuad. "Al-Mouseeka ind Ikhwan al-Safa," Al-Adeeb. (October 1953).

_____. Falsafat Ikhwan al-Safa al-Ijtima'iya wa al-Akhlaqiyah. Baghdad: Ma'arif Press, 1958.

_____. "Madinat Ikhwan al-Safa al-Fadilah," al-Aklam, 3 Baghdad (October 1966).

Behi, Muahmmad al-. "Imamat Ibn Khaldun fi al-Ma'rifa," A'mal Mahrajan Ibn Khaldun. Cairo: National Center for Social Research, 1962.

Ezzat, Abdul Aziz. "Tatawir al-Mujtama al-Bashari 'ind Ibn Khaldun," A'mal Mahrajan Ibn Khaldun, Cairo, 1962.

Farabi, Abu al-Nasr al-. Al-Madina al-Fadilah. Cairo: Nile Press, 1905.

Gallab, Abd al-Karim. "Al-Iltizam al-Ilmi ind Ibn Khaldun," Mahrajan Ibn Khaldun. Casablanca: Dar el-Kitab, 1962.

Hababi, Muhmmed Aziz al-. "Isalat al-Manhajiyah 'ind Ibn Khaldun," Mahrajan Ibn Khaldun. Casablanca: Dar el-Kitab, 1962.

Husri, Sati al-. Dirasat 'an Muqaddimat Ibn Khaldun. Beirut: Kashshaf Press, 1943.

Ibn Khaldun, Abd al-Rahman. Al-Muqaddimah. Beirut: Dar al-Kashshaf, n.d.

_____. Al-Muqaddimah. Beirut: Dar Ihia'a al-Turath al-Arabi, n.d.

_____. Sifà-us Sa'il Litahzib il-Masa'il. Beirut: The Catholic Press, 1959.

Ikhan al-Safa. *Ras'il Ikhwan al-Safa*. Egypt, 1928.

Isa, Ali Ahmed. "Manhaj al-Bahth al-Ilmi ind Ibn Khaldun," *A'mal Mahrajan Ibn Khaldun*. Cairo: National Center for Social Research, 1962.

Jabiri, Muhammad Abid al-. *Al-Asabiyah wa al-Dawla*. Casablanca: Dar al-Thakafa, n.d.

Jum'ah, M. L. *Tarikh Falasifat al-Islam*. Cairo: Ma'arif Press, 1927.

Khadairi, Zainab al-. *Falsafat al-Tareekh ind Ibn Khaldun*. Cairo: Dar al-Thakafa, 1979.

Khalifé, Ignace-Abdo. Introduction to Ibn Khaldun's *Sifa-us-Sa'il Litahzib-il-Masa'il*. Beirut: The Catholic Press, 1959.

Madkoor, Ibrahim B. "Ibn Khaldun: al-Faylasoof," *A'mal Mahrajan Ibn Khaldun*. Cairo: National Center for Social Research, 1962.

Rabi', Muhammad Mahmoud. "Manhaj Ibn Khaldun fi Ilm al-Umran," *L'Egypte Contemporaine*. Cairo, April 1970.

Sa'ati, Hasan al. "Al Manhaj al-Ilmi fi Muqaddamat Ibn Khaldun," *A'mal Mahrajan Ibn Khaldun*. Cairo: National Center for Social Research, 1962.

Shrait, Abdullah. *Al-Fikr al-Akhlaki ind Ibn Khaldun*. Tunis: The National Publishing Co., 1975.

Talibi, Muhammad al-. "Nadariyat Ibn Khaldun fi Sultat al-Dawla," *al-Fikr*, 6 (March 1961).

Wafi, Ali abd al-Wahid. *Abd al-Rahman Ibn Khaldun*. Cairo: Maktabat Misr, 1961.

Wardi, Ali al-. *Mantiq Ibn Khaldun*. Cairo: Institute of Arabic Studies, 1962.

_____. "Ibn Khaldun wa-al-Mujtama al-Arabi," *A'mal Mahrajan Ibn Khaldun*. Cairo: National Center for Social Research, 1962.

Works in Other Languages

Adler, Franz, "The Basic Difficulty of Historical Sociology," *Sociological Quarterly*, 2 (January 1961).

Alam, Manzoor. "Ibn Khaldun's Concept of the Origin, Growth and Decay of Cities," *Islamic Culture*, 23 (April 1960).

Andreski, Stanislav. "Introduction" to A. Comte, *Essential Cours de Philosophie Positive*, trans. by M. Clarke. New York: Barnes and Nobels, 1974.

Aron, Raymond. *Main Currents in Sociological Thought*, Vol. 1. New York: Doubleday, 1968.

Baali, Fuad. *Relation of the People to the Land in Southern Iraq.* Gainesville: University of Florida Press, 1966.

_____. Review of Ali Wardi's *A Study of Iraqi Society, American Sociological Review*, 31 (December 1966).

_____. "Urbanization and Urbanism as a Mode of Life in the Gulf Region of the Southwest Asia." In progress.

_____. and Joseph S. Vandiver. *Urban Sociology*. New York: Appleton-Century-Crofts, 1970.

_____. and Clifton D. Bryant. *Introductory Sociology*. Chicago: Rand McNally, 1970.

_____. and Michael C. Moore. "The Extended Deliberation: Definitions of Sociology," *Sociology and Social Research*, 56 (July 1972).

_____. and J. Brian Price. "Ibn Khaldun and Karl Marx: On Economic and Social Interpretation of History," *Arab Journal for Humanities*, 1 (Winter 1981).

_____. and Ali Wardi. *Ibn Khaldun and Islamic Thought-Styles: A Social Perspective.* Boston: G. K. Hall, 1981.

Barnes, Harry Elmer, ed. *An Introduction to the History of Sociology.* Chicago: University of Chicago Press, 1948.

Barnes, Harry Elmer *et al. Contemporary Social Theory.* New York: D. Appleton-Century, 1940.

Bascom, William. "Urbanization Among the Yoruba," *American Journal of Sociology*, 60 (March 1955).

Becker, Howard and Alvin Boskoff, eds. *Modern Sociological Theory* New York: Dryden Press, 1957.

_____. and Hary Elmer Barnes. *Social Thought from Lore to Science.* New York: Dover Publications, 1961. 3 volumes.

Benet, F. "The Ideology of Islamic Urbanization," *International Journal of Comparative Sociology*, 4 (September 1963).

Benton-Smullyan, Émile. "The Sociologism of Émile Durkheim and His School," in H. E. Barnes, ed. *An Introduction to the History of Sociology.* Chicago: University of Chicago Press, 1948.

Bodin, Jean. *The Six Bookes of a Commonweale,* ed. with introduction by Kenneth Douglas McRae. Cambridge: Harvard University Press, 1962.

Boer, T. J. de. *The History of Philosophy in Islam.* New York: Dover Publications, 1967.

Bottomore, T. B. "The Ideas of the Founding Fathers," *European Journal of Sociology,* 1 (1960).

Bouthoul, Gaston. *Ibn Khaldoun: sa philosophie sociale.* Paris: Libraire Orientaliste Paul Genthner, 1930.

Bridges, John H. *Illustrations of Positivism.* Chicago: The Open Court Publishing Co., 1915.

Busch, Briton Cooper. "Divine Intervention in the Muqaddimah of Ibn Khaldun," *History of Religion,* 7 (May 1968).

Butts, R. Freeman. "Arnold J. Toynbee's Philosophy of History," *Educational Theory,* 22 (Winter 1972).

Cairns, Grace E. *Philosophies of History.* New York: Citadel Press, 1962.

Chambliss, Rollin. *Social Thought from Hammurabi to Comte.* New York: Dryden, 1954.

Cohen, Gerson D. "Ibn Khaldun: Rediscovered Arab Philosopher," *Midstream,* 5 (Summer 1959).

Comte, Auguste. *The Positive Philosophy,* trans. by Harriet Martineau. New York: Calvin Blackard, 1855.

Cooley, Charles Horton. *Social Organization.* New York: Charles Scribner's Sons, 1909.

_____. *Human Nature and the Social Order.* New York: Scribner's 1962.

Douglass, Jack D. and Associates. *Introduction to Sociology: Situations and Structures.* New York: The Free Press, 1973.

Durante, Will. *The Story of Civilization.* New York: Simon and Schuster, 1942.

Durkheim, Émile. *The Division of Labor in Society,* trans. by George Simpson, New York: The Free Press, 1933.

_____. *The Rules of Sociological Method*, trans. by S. A. Solovay and J. H. Mueller, New York: The Free Press, 1938.

_____. *The Elementary Forms of the Religious Life*, trans. by J. Swain. New York: The Free Prss, 1965.

_____. *Montesquieu and Rousseau: Forerunners of Sociology*. Ann Arbor: University of Michigan Press, 1970.

_____. "The Realm of Sociology as a Science," trans. by Everett K. Wilson. *Social Forces*, 59 (June 1981).

Enan, Mohammad Abdullah. *Ibn Khaldun: His Life and Work*. Lahore: Sh. Muhammad Ashraf, 1969.

Ezzat, Abd el-Aziz. *Ibn Khaldoun et sa science sociale*. Cairo: Universite de Fouad, 1947.

Farrukh, Umar. *The Arab Genius in Science and Philosophy*, trans. by John B. Hardie. Washington, D. C.: The American Council of Learned Societies, 1954.

Fischel, Walter J. *Ibn Khaldun in Egypt: His Public Functions and Historical Research (1382-1406) — A Study in Islamic Historiography*. Berkeley and Los Angeles: University of California Press, 1967.

Fischer, Claude S. "The Effect of Urban Life on Traditional Values," *Social Forces*, 53 (March 1975).

Flint, Robert. *History of the Philosophy of History*. New York: Charles Scribner's Sons, 1894.

Gellner, Ernest. *Muslim Society*. Cambridge: Cambridge University Press, 1981.

Gibb, Hamilton A. R. "The Islamic Background of Ibn Khaldun's Political Theory," in S. J. Shaw and W. R. Polk, eds. *Studies on the Civilization of Islam*. Boston: Beacon Press, 1962.

Gré, Gerard O. C. de. *Society and Ideology: An Inquiry into the Sociology of Knowledge*. New York: Columbia University Press Bookstore, 1943.

Grupp, S. E. "The Sociology of Gabriel Tarde," *Sociology and Social Research*, 52 (July 1968).

Gumplowicz, Ludwig. *Outlines of Sociology*, ed. by Irving L. Horowitz. New York: Paine-Whitman Publishers, 1963.

Heberle, Rudolf. "The Application of Fundamental Concepts in Rural Community Studies," *Rural Sociology,* 6 (September 1941).

————. "The Sociology of Georg Simmel: The Forms of Social Interaction," in Harry Elmer Barnes, ed. *An Introduction to the History of Sociology.* Chicago: University of Chicago Press, 1948.

————. "Ferdinand Tönnies' Contributions to the Sociology of Political Parties," *American Journal of Sociology,* 61 (May 1955).

————. "Preface," in F. Tönnies, *Gemeinschaft and Gesellschaft.* English trans. East Lansing: Michigan State University Press, 1957.

Hitti, Philip K. *History of the Arabs,* 3rd ed. London: Macmillan, 1946.

————. *Makers of Arab History,* New York: Harper, 1968.

Horowitz, Irving Louis: "Introduction," in Ludwig Gumplowicz, *Outline of Sociology.* New York: Paine-Whitman Publishers, 1963.

Hourani, Albert. *Arabic Thought in the Liberal Age: 1798-1939.* London: Oxford University Press, 1962.

Hussein, Taha. *Étude analytique et critique de la philosophie sociale d'Ibn Khaldoun.* Paris: A. Pedone, 1917.

Ibn Khaldun, Abd al-Rahman. *The Muqaddimah: An Introduction to History,* trans. by Franz Rosenthal. Princeton: Princeton University Press, 1967. 3 Volumes.

Irving, T. B. "A Fourteenth-Century View of Language," in J. Kritzeck and R. B. Winder, eds. *The World of Islam.* London: MacMillan, 1960.

Israel, Joachim. *Alienation: From Marx to Modern Sociology.* Boston: Allyn and Bacon, 1971.

Issawi, Charles. *An Arab Philosophy of History: Selections from the Prolegomena of Ibn Khaldun of Tunis, 1332-1406.* London: John Murray, 1950.

Lacoste, Yves. *Ibn Khaldoun: naissance de l'histoire passe du tiers monde,* Arabic trans. by M. Sulaiman. Beirut: Ibn Khaldun House, 1973.

Lahbabi, Muhammad Aziz. *Ibn Khaldun: Presentation, Choix de texts, bibliographie.* Paris: Seghers, 1968.

Lewis, Oscar. "Urbanization Without Breakdown: A Case Study," *The Scientific Monthly,* 75 (July 1952).

Lichtenstadter, Ilse. *Islam and the Modern Age*. New York: Bookman Associates, 1958.

Lukes, Steven. *Émile Durkheim – His Life and Work: A Historical and Critical Study*. New York: Penguin Books, 1973.

Macdonald, Duncan B. *The Religious Attitudes and Life in Islam*. Chicago: University of Chicago Press, 1909.

Machiavelli, Niccolò. *The Prince*, trans. by L. Ricci. New York: The New American Library, 1952.

Mahdi, Muhsin. *Ibn Khaldun's Philosophy of History*. Chicago: University of Chicago Press, 1964.

_____. "Ibn Khaldun," *International Social Science Encyclopedia*. New York: Macmillan, 1968.

Mannheim, Karl. *Ideology and Utopia*. New York: Harcourt, Brace, 1936.

Markham, Felix. "Introduction" in Henri de Saint-Simon, *Social Organization, The Science of Man and Other Writings*. New York: Harper Torchbooks, 1964.

Martindale, Don. "Prefatory Remarks: The Theory of the City," in Max Weber, *The City*. New York: The Free Press, 1958.

Marx, Karl and Frederick Engels. *The Communist Manifesto*. New York: International Publishers, 1964.

McKinney, John C. "Application of Gemeinschaft and Gesellschaft as Related to Other Typologies," in F. Tönnies, *Gemeinschaft and Gesellschaft*. English translation. East Lansing: Michigan State University Press, 1957.

Mead, George H. *Mind, Self and Society*. Chicago: University of Chicago Press, 1934.

Michels, Roberto. *First Lectures in Political Sociology*. New York: Harper Torchbooks, 1965.

Mills, C. Wright. "Language, Logic, and Culture," *American Sociological Review*, 4 (October 1939).

_____. *The Sociological Imagination*. London: Oxford University Press, 1959.

Miner, Horace. "The Folk-Urban Continuum," *American Sociological Review*, 17 (October 1952).

Montesquieu, Charles de Secondat. *The Spirit of the Laws*, trans. by T. Nugent. New York: Hafner, 1949.

Nashat, Mohammad Ali. "Ibn Khaldoun: Pioneer Economist," *L'Egypte Contemporaine*, 35 (1945).

Nicholson, Reynold A. *A Literary History of the Arabs.* Cambridge: Cambridge University Press, 1930.

Nisbet, Robert A. *Émile Durkheim.* Englewood Cliffs. N. J.: Prentice-Hall, 1965.

Nour, Mohamed Abdel Monem. "An Analytical Study of the Sociological Thought of Ibn Khaldun," dissertation. University of Kentucky, 1953.

Oppenheimer, Franz. *The State.* New York: Vanguard Press, 1922.

Pellegrin, Roland J. "The Study of Social Change and Theory," *Sociological Spectrum*, 2 (July–December 1982).

Perrucci, Robert and D. D. Knudsen. *Sociology.* St. Paul, Minn.: West Publishing Co., 1986.

Pompa, Leon. "Vico's Science," *History and Theory*, 10 (1971).

Popenoe, David. *Sociology.* Englewood Cliff, N. J.: Prentice-Hall, 1983.

Qudsi, Obaidullah. "Ibn Khaldun ur Auguste Comte ka tkabla Mutala'a," unpublished manuscript. In Urdu.

Rabi', Muhammad Mahmoud. *The Political Theory of Ibn Khaldun.* Leiden: E. J. Brill, 1967.

Ritter, Hellmut. "Irrational Solidarity Groups: A Socio-Psychological Study in Connection with Ibn Khaldun," *Oriens*, 1 (1948).

Rosenthal, Erwin, I. J. "Ibn Khaldun: A North African Muslim Thinker of the Fourteenth Century," *Bulletin of the John Rylands Library*, 24 (1940).

_____. *Islam in the Modern National State.* Cambridge: Cambridge University Press, 1965.

Rosenthal, Franz. "Introduction" to Ibn Khaldun, *The Muqaddimah: An Introduciton to History*, trans. by Franz Rosenthal. Princeton: Princeton University Press, 1967.

Runes, D. D. *Dictionary of Philosophy.* Paterson, N. J.: Littlefield, Adams and Co., 1961.

Saint-Simon, Henri de. *Social Organization, The Science of Man.* New York: Harper Torchbooks, 1964.

Sarton, George, *Introduction to the History of Science,* Vol. 3. Baltimore, Md.: Williams and Wilkins, 1948.

Schaefer, R. T. and R. P. Lamm. *Sociology.* New York: McGraw-Hill, 1983.

Schmidt, Nathaniel. *Ibn Khaldun: Historian, Sociologist and Philosopher.* New York: Columbia University Press, 1930.

Sherwani, Haron Khan. *Studies in Muslim Political Thought and Administration.* Lahore: Sh. Muhammad Ashraf, 1959.

Shiber, Saba G. "Ibn Khaldun: An Early Town Planner," *Middle East Forum,* 38 (March 1962).

Simmel, Georg. *The Sociology of Georg Simmel,* ed. by K. H. Wolff. New York: The Free Press, 1950.

_____. *Conflict and the Web of Group-Affiliation.* Glencoe, Ill.: The Free Press, 1955.

_____. *On Individuality and Social Forms.* Chicago: University of Chicago Press, 1971.

Simon, Heinrich. *Ibn Khalduns Wissenschaft von der Menschlichen Kultur.* Leipzig, 1959.

Smelser, Neil J. "Sociology and the Other Social Sciences," in P. F. Lazarsfeld *et al, The Uses of Sociology.* New York: Basic Books, 1967.

Sorokin, Pitirim A. *Contemporary Sociological Theory.* New York: Harper, 1928.

_____. *The Crisis of Our Age.* New York: E. P. Dutton, 1946.

_____. "Forward," in F. Tönnies, *Gemeinschaft and Gesellschaft.* English trans. East Lansing: Michigan State University Press, 1957.

_____. *Society, Culture, and Personality.* New York: Cooper Square Publishers, 1962.

_____. *Sociological Theories of Today.* New York: Harper and Row, 1966.

————, Carle C. Zimmerman, and Charles Galpin, eds. *A Systematic Source Book in Rural Sociology*, Vol. 1. Minneapolis: University of Minnesota Press, 1930.

Spencer, Herbert, *The Study of Sociology*. New York: D. Appleton, 1895.

————. *The Principles of Sociology*. New York: D. Appleton, 1895.

Spengler, Joseph. "Economic Thought of Islam: Ibn Khaldun," *Comparative Studies in Society and History*, 6 (1963–1964).

Spengler, Oswald. *The Decline of the West*, trans. by Charles Atkinson. New York: Alfred A. Knopf, 1932.

Spuler, B. "Ibn Khaldoun The Historian," *A'mal Mahrajan Ibn Khaldun*. Cairo: National Center for Social Research, 1962.

Spykman, Nicholas J. *The Social Theory of Georg Simmel*. New York: Atherton Press, 1966.

Sumner, William G. and A. G. Keller. *Science of Society*, Vol. 1. New York: Yale University Press, 1927.

Thakeb, Fahed Thakeb al-. *Family-Kin Relationships in Contemporary Kuwaiti Society*. Kuwait: Annals of the Faculty of Arts, Kuwait University, Vol. 3, 1982.

Thorns, D. C. "The Growth of Sociological Method," *New Directions in Sociology*. Totowa, N. J.: Rowman and Littlefield, 1976.

Timasheff, Nicholas S. *Sociological Theory: Its Nature and Growth*. New York: Random House, 1967.

Tönnies, Ferdinand. *On Social Ideas and Ideologies*, ed. and trans. by E. G. Jacoby. New York: Harper and Row, 1974.

————. *Gemeinschaft and Gesellschaft*, English trans. East Lansing: Michigan State University Press, 1957.

Toynbee, Arnold J. *A Study of History*, Vol. 3. New York: Oxford University Press, 1962.

Turgot, Ann Robert Jacques. *On Progress, Sociology and Economics*, trans. and ed. by Robert L. Meek. Cambridge: Cambridge University Press, 1973.

Ülken, Hilmi zia. "Ibn Khaldoun, Initiateur de la sociologie," *A'mal Mahrajan Ibn Khaldun*. Cairo: National Center for Social Research, 1962.

Venable, V. *Human Nature: The Marxian View.* New York: Alfred A. Knopf, 1945.

Vico, Giambattista. *The New Science,* trans. by T. G. Bergin and M. H. Fisch. Ithaca, N. Y.: Cornell University Press, 1968.

Walzer, Richard. "Aspects of Islamic Political Thought: Al-Farabi and Ibn Xaldun," *Oriens,* 16 (1963).

Watt, W. M. *Islamic Political Thought: The Basic Concepts.* Edinburgh: The University Press, 1968.

Weatley, P. "The Concept of Urbanism," in P. J. Ucko *et al.,* eds. *Man, Settlement and Urbanism.* London and Cambridge, Mass.: Schenkman Publishing Co., 1972.

Weber, Max. *From Max Weber: Essays in Sociology,* trans. by H. H. Gerth and C. Wright Mills. New York: Oxford University Press, 1946.

_____. *The Theory of Social and Economic Organization.* Glencoe, Ill.: The Free Press, 1947.

_____. *The City,* trans. and ed. by Don Martindale and Gertrud Neuwirth. New York: The Free Press, 1958.

_____. *Sociology of Religion.* London: Methuen, 1966.

White, Hayden V. "Ibn Khaldun in World Philosophy of History," *Comparative Studies in Society and History,* 2 (1959-1960).

Wiese, Leopold von. *Systematic Sociology.* New York: Arno Press, 1974.

Will, Edouard. Review of G. Nebel's *Sokrates. Revue Historique* (October-December, 1970).

Willer, Judith. "The Implications of Durkheim's Philosophy of Science," *Kansas Journal of Sociology,* 4 (Fall 1969).

Wirth, Louis. "Urbanism as a Way of Life," *American Journal of Sociology,* 41 (July 1938).

INDEX

CPSIA information can be obtained at www.ICGtesting.com
Printed in the USA
LVOW07s0004120215

426668LV00001B/64/P